Border Co

Border Collie Dog Care Manual

*Border Collie Temperament, Pros and Cons,
Health, Care, Training, Costs and Medical
Concerns.*

By

Jacob Highcombe

Published by IMB Publishing - 2015

Table Of Contents

Chapter 1: Introduction

There are more than 150 different breeds of dogs categorized into various groups like the herding group, sporting group, toy group, non-sporting group, working group, small breeds, large breeds and more. Each of the breeds has their own set of characteristics and traits.

Border Collie is an energetic, medium sized, working dog. It has an athletic appearance and displays agility and style in equal measure with strength and soundness. Its muscular body gives out the impression of endless endurance and effortless movements. The Border Collie has alert and keen expressions and is known for its intelligence.

This amazing dog is an unspoiled and natural working sheep dog. It is specifically bred to accomplish tricky tasks and when trained effectively, can easily manage any training or work. The Border Collie needs a lot of dedication and time to train and exercise, and is usually not recommended for first time dog owners. However, these dogs make extremely useful and loving pets.

Before you make the decision of adopting a Border Collie, there are several things you have to first consider and evaluate. It is best to carefully assess all aspects instead of opting for gut-instinct purchases!

You need to ask you self whether a Border Collie is the right dog for you. Are there other breeds that will be better for you? Will the Border Collie be properly taken care of under your care?

If you want to know more about this breed, its care, training and other details, then this is the perfect book for you. This book has all the information you will need to take good care of your Border Collie and enjoy to the fullest with this extremely intelligent and adorable dog.

Chapter 2: Border Collie – Scotch Sheep Dog

A dog is undoubtedly the most amazing pet you could get. Dogs are loyal, faithful and try their level best to keep their owners happy. They are unconditionally loving companions and love spending time with you. Most important of all, they do whatever they can to protect their owners!

If you have been thinking about getting a pet, then a dog is one of the best options you have. There are a few dogs that are quite bright and intelligent and a Border Collie is known as the most intelligent dog breeds of all time.

It's known for its hypnotic, fixed and intimidating stare and is considered as the most challenging to live with. They have an obsessive zeal to work and combined with their intensity and superior intellect – this is considered as their most impressive feature. This loving dog is a workaholic and needs constant action.

If you are considering adopting a Border Collie as your pet, then there are a lot of things you need to know first. This book is a great compilation of all you need to know about a Border Collie. Let's get started!

1. *Amazing Facts about the Border Collie Breed*

Let's begin with some facts about this breed. Here are some amazing ones you should know about Border Collies:

They Originate from Scotland and England

Border Collie is a relatively new name for a farm and shepherd dog. The breed originally developed in the border linking Scotland and England – hence the name.

They are Considered as the Best Herding Breed

These dogs are super skilled at various jobs and tasks yet at heart they are sheep herders. They are usually employed as sheep dogs and also compete in different herding competitions.

They Are Well-Known For Their Intelligence

Border Collies have been ranked as the smartest dog breed in the world. Their intelligence is the reason why they are keen and excited to perform complex tasks like herding sheep and performing agility courses. However, they are just as happy playing fetch as they need action and are eager to constantly move their body.

They Can Handle Complex Tasks Aside From Herding

This breed is born to herd. However, their eagerness to please their owners, their drive and intelligence usually results in them getting employed for several other tasks and jobs. Border Collies make excellent medical alert dogs, search and rescue dogs and therapy dogs.

Their Lines Can Be Traced Back To A Single Dog

Old Hemp is the father of all Border Collies. The dog lived from 1893 to 1901 and started herding when it was merely 6 weeks old. It showed natural talent for work and a unique herding style, which was less aggressive and quieter as compared to other sheep dogs, without losing any effectiveness of the task. The temperament and ability of this dog inspired the codification and creation of the breed of Border Collies.

They Are Great Actors

It is probably due to their workaholic nature and intelligence that Border Collies have been cast in various TV shows and movies. Most famous examples include Mad About You, Little House on the Prairie, Babe and Babe: Pig in the City.

A Border Collie Holds A World Record!

Striker is a Border Collie that holds a Guinness World Record for "Fastest Car Window Opened By A Dog" Striker opened the window of the non-electric car in 11.34 seconds with its nose and paw. This record was set in Quebec, Canada, in September 2004.

2. Brief History of Border Collies

Border Collies are descended from the landrace Collies widely found in British Isles. The term 'Border Collie' was first used by James Ried, Secretary of the International Sheep Dog Society (ISDS) in 1915. This term was used to distinguish the dogs registered by ISDS from Kennel Club's Collie.

Unlike majority of the other dog breeds, Border Collies are still being bred, valued and used for their original purpose – to herd sheep. Aside from herding, this dog breed has been valued for other reasons as well like companionship, search and rescue, service, agility and obedience. They have always been valued and bred for their capabilities instead of their appearances.

Today, Border Collies are recognized as leading herding dogs. Their intelligence and herding abilities lead people to breed them for maintaining working standards.

Chapter 3: Breeding

What a dog becomes is usually dependent on the way it is bred. This is true for all breeds of dogs. Breeding is the primary stage of ensuring the well-being and health of a dog. Breeding dogs is not an easy process as it involves considering and handling various particulars simultaneously.

If you are looking for a healthy and happy Border Collie, then you need to locate a reputable breeder and also carefully consider some other aspects.

1. Finding a Reputable Breeder

Even though a reputable breeder can't ensure a lifelong healthy dog, they can easily offer prospective Border Collie owner with a lot of helpful information regarding the dog. It is essential for you to inquire from the breeder about the health, care, cost, and even about the parents of the Border Collie before you make the final decision about getting the dog.

A good breeder will have the dog tested for eye, thyroid and hip problems. You must also ask about possible congenital problems that the parents of the dog might have had. Responsible breeders don't simply give away dogs to individuals who come up with the cash; they take good care of the puppies and give them to individuals who they believe will take good care of them.

In many cases, unsuspecting potential dog owners purchase their dogs from breeders who are simply in it for the cash or from the puppy mills. This often results in temperament or health problems with the dog. This is the reason why it is essential to look for a responsible and reputed breeder.

Here are a few tips to locate such a breeder:

- A reputed breeder might always ask you to sign a contract that includes certain care conditions and state that in case you are unable to meet those conditions, the dog will be reclaimed. This shows that the breeder is not merely in for the money but actually cares for the well-being of the dogs.

- A good breeder will only give you the puppy when it is between 8 to 12 weeks old. This is because it is crucial for the puppy to get sufficient time to socialize with its littermates and mother, and mature.

- Good breeders are more than willing to answer any concerns and questions you might have regarding the dogs. They will even ask you some questions to ensure that you are capable of handling a dog.

- You must always observe the breeder's premises. Is the kennel/house properly cleaned? Does it smell? Are all the puppies and dogs taken care of properly? Are they friendly, lively and well fed? Look out for any signs of illness like skin sores, lethargy, coughing, runny eyes or nose and the signs for malnutrition like protruding rib cages.

- Observe the interaction between the breeder and the dogs. Does the breeder seem to care genuinely for the dogs? Do the dogs shy away from the breeder?

2. Border Collie's Parents

It is important to meet the parents of the Border Collie that you are about to adopt, as this will help you learn a lot about the demeanor and temperament of the puppy. The Border Collie's temperament and personality will be a mixture of whatever environment they live in initially and the genes inherited from the parents.

It is best to visit the breeder a few times and observe the parents before you buy the puppy. Interact with the puppies and ask different questions regarding the dog as this will not only help you in getting to know about the breeder's sincerity, but also the temperament and personality that your puppy will probably have once it has grown up after spending time with its parents.

The parents of your puppy will give you a good idea about what you should expect from your puppy. However, this isn't a guarantee for good companionship and relations.

In case the parents aren't available on site, you can ask questions related to them from the breeder. This will give you an idea about their temperament. Remember to inquire about their medical and health records. Registration and documentation papers are another effective way of assessing the well-being and other details about the parents.

3. Some Questions to Ask Yourself

Adopting a pet is a big commitment. It is essential that you ensure that you are prepared to handle such a big responsibility. In order to determine whether you are ready to take care of a dog, ask yourself the following questions:

Are you really prepared to take full care of a dog?

Are you in the right state of mind to handle this responsibility? Are you usually assertive and calm? Are you patient enough to tend to the needs of a dog?

Why do you want a dog?

Take your time with this one and answer honestly. Your behavior will be a reflection of your dog's behavior. Are you organized and neat? Do you follow rules and boundaries?

How much time do you think you will be able to give to your dog every day?

As compared to cats, dogs need more attention and time. Your dog will need undivided attention from you. If your dog doesn't get the daily dosage of interaction and affection, then they will have increased chances of behavioral problems, obesity and anxiety. Your dog needs snuggles and cuddles, regular walking and playing, to stay healthy and happy.

Do you have enough support from your family and friends so that they can take care of your dog if you are traveling or working late?

If you simply confine your dog indoors when you are away or in case of any emergency, this can lead to bladder infections and behavioral problems. It is best to look for people you trust, who can care for your dog while you are away or look for daycare, sitters and boarding facilities for your dog before you actually adopt them.

Are you sure about the dog breed you are about to adopt?

Have you considered your lifestyle, your personality, space restriction, children and amount of time you can give before you decided upon the dog breed? Is a Border Collie right for your household?

Will you be able to afford your dog's safety and health?

Adopting or owning a dog costs much more than just the adoption fee. You must have enough for neutering, spaying, veterinary care, food, microchipping and other costs.

Will you be able to handle the health challenges of your dog?

Allergies, fleas and sudden medical problems are a few of the health related problems that are faced by dog owners. Are you prepared to handle them?

Are you ready to properly train your dog?

Not training the pet properly is one of the common reasons why many pet owners return their pets to the shelters. Are you willing to make efforts to train your dog? Basic training is crucial to develop a good communication between the dog and the owner, as it helps in strengthening the overall relationship.

Have you pet-proofed your home?

You must make your home safe before you bring your dog home. Pet proofing your home includes putting away dangerous holiday decorations safely, sealing your garbage cans tightly, storing away deadly plants, toxic food and other household items that can prove dangerous for your pet.

Do you have enough space to have a dog?

Ensure that you have enough space for your dog to roam about freely. If you want a Border Collie but you live in a small apartment, then this can be a problem as Border Collies need a lot of space to run about. You must also check with your land lord first before you adopt a dog.

Are all your family members ready for a dog?

Are your spouse or your parents and siblings ready to care for a dog? If your children are still toddlers, will you be able to tend to the needs of both, your child and your pet? Do you have other pets? Will there be a problem if you introduce another pet in the house?

4. Some Questions to Ask the Breeder

When selecting a dog as a pet, money is never an important consideration. The ethics and support of the breeder as well as the health of the dog is one of the biggest priorities. When selecting the right breeder, you must ask them the following questions. All the answers you receive from the breeder should be able to satisfy you and make you feel confident.

Are the parents of the dog certified?

Many of the breeds are usually at risk of genetic problems like eye conditions, heart issues or hip problems. The majority of these diseases are inherited which means that they can be passed on to the puppies. Good breeders get their dogs evaluated and tested for such diseases and get them certified by a specialist. It is

12

best to know more about the breed, parentage and common problems.

What is the size of the parents of the dog?

This will give you an idea about how big your puppy will get. Will the size be suitable for the place you are currently living in?

Can I meet the parents of the dog?

This will give you an idea about the temperament of the puppy so that you can determine whether you will be able to handle the dog properly.

Has the puppy been socialized?

Was the puppy around other dogs? Was it around people? Proper socialization of a puppy means that the puppy has socialized with other puppies and dogs of various types, ages and sizes. This also means that the puppy has interacted with humans as well. This will indicate that the puppy will be well adjusted in your home.

Has the puppy been vaccinated?

Which vaccines has it had and how many shots has it received? Is the puppy due for other shots?

Have you gotten the puppy dewormed?

Each and every puppy is born with worms and it is recommended that the puppy gets dewormed as soon as possible.

Did any of the puppies in the litter fall sick?

If yes, then what were the signs, treatment and diagnosis?

Has the puppy visited the veterinarian?

Has the puppy been examined and has it been declared as healthy by the veterinarian? If not, then what problems does it have? Is it on medication?

Is there any guarantee?

Is the breeder offering you any guarantee? What if the dog has some severe illness, then what will the breeder do? This might be a difficult question but it needs to be addressed before the adoption, rather than after.

Do you have any recommendations?

Ask your breeder to provide you with a few recommendations from the dog owners they sold to. Call up those references and inquire about the service they received and the health of the dog. Are they happy with their dogs? Have they faced any problems?

Do you have a breeder's contract?

Is there a need for a breeder's contract? If yes, then does your breeder have a contract? Will the breeder be able to take the puppy back in case you aren't able to keep it?

Tell me about the dog's family history?

Ask questions related to the family history of the dog so that you get to know more about it. For example; their life expectancy, what are the common causes of death etc. This will be essential to monitor your dog as it gets older.

What are you currently feeding the dog?

You will have to continue feeding the same food to the dog initially and gradually change the diet if you want to reduce the risk of any gastrointestinal problems.

Will you provide me the health certificate of the puppy?

Will you receive the health certificate issued by the veterinarian for the puppy? Will you need a certificate of sale for the puppy?

5. Some Questions to Expect From the Breeder

Reputed breeders try hard to find the best home for all the puppies and dogs. This is the reason why they might ask a few questions regarding you, your home and your life before they make the decision of giving you one of the puppies. This is because they want to ensure that you are capable enough to take on the responsibilities of a dog.

Here are a few questions you can expect a breeder to ask you:

Have you ever taken care of a dog? Which dog breed did you have before? How long did you have the dog for?

There are certain breeds that are unsuitable for first time dog owners. Some dogs require the owner to be a little experienced in handling the dogs and training them.

Do you have children? What are their ages?

Certain dog breeds are amazing with children while others aren't able to get along well with them.

Do you live in an apartment or a house? Do you have enough space for a dog to live in freely? Are you allowed to have dogs in your apartment?

Some dogs are completely fine with confined spaces but other dogs need a lot of space to wander around and stretch.

Do you have any other pets?

Certain dogs are aggressive towards other pets while some get along really well with them.

Is your yard fenced?

It is highly recommended that you don't allow your dog out unattended and no dog must be confined merely by an electronic fence. Such fences might prevent your dog from getting out but may not be able to prevent trespassing children or other animals from getting in.

Do you exercise?

Certain breeds including Border Collies, Retrievers, Dalmatians and Australian Shepherds need a jog or a walk everyday for a mile or so, in order to satisfy their psychological and physical needs for exercise.

Are you aware about the dog laws in your country, state and community?

No responsible dog breeder will want to give their dog to an owner who doesn't abide by the confinement and leash laws.

Are you planning to obedience train your dog?

This is an important question especially if you are planning on adopting dogs like Dobermans, German Shepherds, Boxers, Rottweilers, Akitas etc. If such dogs aren't trained, this could result in severe behavioral problems.

Will you be able to handle the costs of having a pet?

Do you know the financial cost of dog care including good quality food, neutering and spaying, boarding, license fees etc?

Are you prepared to handle the responsibility of a dog?

Do you realize that you will be responsible for the care of another living creature solely dependent on you for the rest of its life? Are you ready for it?

If you are able to positively answer all these questions, possibly even more, and satisfy the breeder that you are indeed responsible and aware of the responsibilities of having a dog; then you will be considered as a good prospect for their dog.

They will further assess your behavior with the dogs and your attitude towards other animals and even children, before they make the decision of giving you their puppy.

Chapter 4: Characteristics

Now it is time to know some more crucial details about Border Collies. It is essential to understand what exactly you are getting in to when you get this breed. Furthermore, these details will help you in taking better care of your pet once you adopt it.

Here is all that you need to know about the main characteristics of a Border Collie:

1. Origin of Border Collies

Originally, Border Collie was known as "Scotch Sheep Dog". It originates from Northumberland near the borders of England and Scotland. This breed's ancestors were used to herd reindeer by the Vikings. Border Collies are named as workaholics due to their sheer love and drive to work. It has a sharp eye which can hypnotize the cattle. This dog has a knack of mastering any kind of herd merely by bending down and using its intense gaze to mesmerize the animals. It is considered as the most trainable breed among dogs and it serves great as a bomb detection and narcotics detection dog.

Border Collie is a high performer in competitive obedience, performing tricks, Flyball, search and rescue, police work, agility and obedience. These dogs can also be successfully trained as guide dogs for the blind. They are also extremely helpful in providing assistance to handicapped individuals. This breed was first recognized in 1995.

2. Main Physical Features

Border Collie's head is quite similar to that of Australian Cattle dogs, with a noticeable stop, longer and faintly tapered muzzle and short hair covering the entire face. Their eyes are alert and well-set, continuously scanning their surroundings.

When the dog is extremely focused, its ears are fully erect but otherwise they are generally half pricked. The hair on the head is sleek and short giving a somewhat roundish appearance to the face. There is usually a lot of fringing along the Border Collie's cheeks and the ears.

The body of Border Collie is longer as compared to its height. Its back is leveled or sloping a little towards the hind quarters. It is well developed but isn't cobby or heavy, while the legs are boned moderately and aren't heavy or stocky.

The front legs of the Border Collie are straight and well positioned. The hind legs are muscular and strong and might also have hocks that slightly turn in. The tail has a gentle curl near the hocks and usually goes down while the dog is in work mode.

Border Collie's movement is naturally graceful and jaunty. However, when they are getting ready to work or herd, they typically crouch and appear to be slinking across the ground. This breed has the ability of changing direction while running rather quickly and they are incredibly athletic in both jumping and running.

3. Coat Colors

The coat of a dog is undoubtedly one of its key features. Border Collie's coats are in different colors.

White and Black

The most common coat color of Border Collies is white and black. As with every other color, the pattern appears in a white blaze which covers the top of the head and a little area on the neck. The tail end has some white color. The dog's forelegs are white usually till the elbows and it has white colored socks on the hind legs. The rest of the coat is in black.

White and Chocolate Brown

This is also a common coat color, though not as common as black and white. The pattern is as same as the black and white one but the black is replaced with chocolate brown color.

White / Light Brown (White / Yellow)

This is a rare color in Border Collies. The markings and patterns are as the same as white and black dogs. There are several shades of this color and are sometimes called yellow, red, cream and blond depending on the areas.

White and Blue

The black color of the Border Collie becomes a little diluted and appears bluish grey. It is also known as slate. This too, is a rare coat color for Border Collie.

White and Sable

This is a darker reddish white color. Sable refers to a pattern in which certain parts of the hair appear darker than the rest.

Tricolor

Brownish markings appear outside of the colored parts, especially above the eyes. The intensity and width of these markings must vary from dog to dog. This pattern is usually combined with merle, chocolate brown, blue and black.

Saddle Pattern

This coat color is similar to the tricolor but the brown markings are bigger and intense. The darker is sometimes limited to a saddle patch on the back.

Blue Merle

This effect is seen in many other breeds as well. The patch of black color is replaced by different shades of black and grey patterns. If the parents of the dog are merle then the offspring can inherit this coat trait from both parents and become 'double merles'.

Sable Merle

It is genetically achievable to create a sable merle but tricky in practice. This pattern in the coat can only be viewed on the puppies. Once the dog grows its final coat, the merle markings are hard to see.

White Face

It is not actually a pattern or a color but such dogs usually have a complete white face or have bigger patches of white color on the face and head.

Mottled

In this pattern, the dog has freckles or spots on the face or other parts of the coat. This might be combined with different colors as well. This pattern is also known as ticked.

4. Weight and Height

Border Collies are medium sized dogs and typically weigh around 30 to 45 pounds when fully grown. Their weight is less than one pound at the time of birth. Afterwards, they go through a miraculous transformation in weight and height. A Border Collie has a dramatic growth rate from newborn stage to puppyhood, plateauing in late adolescence.

Newborns

When a Border Collie is born, it is extremely tiny. It is like a compact package of bones, skin and organs. Its birth weight is between 7 to 14 ounces. The speed of weight gain in Border Collie puppies differs but each puppy steadily gains weight.

It does lose a significant amount of water weight within 24 hours of its birth but immediately starts to put on some weight after that. In the first week, their weight doubles. Afterwards, they gain ½ to 1½ ounce every day till they are 6 weeks of age.

Puppies

Within the first 6 weeks, the now 3 to 6 pounds Border Collie puppy quadrupled their weight at birth. When they have reached puppyhood, the Border Collie puppies start gaining about 3 to 4 pounds of weight each week till they are 14 weeks old. At that point, this weight gain speed levels down a little and the dog starts gaining one pound each week till they are 6 months old. It is important to bear in mind that each puppy gains weight at a different rate.

Adolescence

Once a Border Collie reaches this stage, they have attained their full height between 18 to 22 inches and have achieved their full weight of around 21 to 35 pounds. The adolescence stage of the Border Collie usually involves rangy, tall and gangly pups that aren't quite filled out. At this stage, the majority of the dogs ravenously eat in order to support their incredibly high metabolism and energy levels. Whilst your dog will continue to gain some more weight all through this stage, it will be far slower as compared to in puppyhood.

An adolescent Border Collie is hyper metabolic which means there is bound to be a struggle to keep the weight on. It is recommended to maintain a calorie dense high quality food diet for the dog so that it can properly support its never ending movement and activity.

Adults

An adult Border Collie possess a glossy and thick coat, have intuitive and intelligent eyes and a lithe physique. The adult dog has gradually filled out and has passed the awkward adolescent stage. Now it is has become a highly beautiful dog.

The adult Border Dog weights between 30 to 45 pounds and it is no more a struggle for them to maintain their weight. An active adult border can easily maintain its weight but a senior border will have to struggle to ensure the weight doesn't go upward.

5. Life Expectancy

The life expectancy of Border Collies is around 10 to 17 years. The average life expectancy is 12 years. The life span of other breeds of same size as the Border Collies is around 12 to 13 years. The prevalent causes of death among Border Collies include cerebral vascular afflictions, old age and cancer.

6. Litter Size

The litter size of Border Collies is between 4 to 8 puppies. The average is around 6. In many cases, this number might be smaller or larger as per the condition of the mother.

7. Personality

Border Collie's personality isn't as malleable as its physical characteristics. However, each dog has its own unique personality features. As a whole, Border Collies are quite loving and gentle. They are also extremely protective and can make great watchdogs.

The distinctive feature of this breed is that it is a watcher and observer. The dog will observe what its owner is doing, what the rest of the family is doing and what the other animals around it are doing. This breed learns through observation which is the reason they make outstanding working and herding dogs.

Early socialization and training is significant for Border Collies as they are mostly independent and can become aggressive if not properly trained. The male dogs tend to get more aggressive towards other male dogs if not trained but then again the nature of each dog varies. Socialization from an early age can minimize or eradicate this trait.

Border Collies are extremely intelligent and also very sensitive as they can easily detect even a slight change of tone in their owner's voice. These dogs shouldn't be given negative training or harsh punishments as for them positive training works extremely well. If your puppy is very sensitive then it is essential that it is carefully socialized so that it doesn't become timid when it is an adult.

It is a perfect dog for those individuals who are ready to work on their dogs every day – ensuring they get proper exercise and interaction with the owner on regular basis. It is important to learn about both personality as well as physical traits of your Border Collie as it will ensure that you make all the right decisions from selecting the dog to ensuring it stays happy and healthy.

8. Intelligence

It is a well known fact that the Border Collie is the most intelligent breed of dogs there is in the world. It is a dog that keeps its owner on their toes, as it constantly needs some physical activity.

Border Collies need a good amount of exercise every day and must be assigned a job to keep them from getting into trouble because a Border Collie that is bored can resort to doing pretty much anything to keep itself entertained.

Border Collies never stop thinking and are known to stay ahead of their owner. One can see the wheels turning in its head as it enthusiastically continues to search and observe its surroundings. This dog loves to learn and if you take out enough time and make some effort then your dog can learn to do just about anything.

It is important to be careful about what you teach your Border Collie as it is intelligent enough to teach itself things that you wouldn't want it to learn.

This dog thrives on praise! Yes, you will have to keep praising your dog to keep it happy. However, Border Collies are quite stubborn and are bound to try outsmarting their owners if they are given an upper hand.

It is essential for the owner to be aware and understand the level of intelligence of this dog to keep it under control. An untrained and bored Border Collie can develop grave behavioral issues, which means it won't make a good family pet.

This dog might be sensitive to sudden and loud noises and might try herding just about anything that moves before them. This includes livestock, cars, cats, other dogs, kids and even its owner.

Border Collies are observant and smart. They are able to detect variations in voice tones and how commands are being given to them and even observe how their owner uses hands in the training activities. This dog can detect and spot small changes that usually go undetected by the owners. It is essential to maintain consistency when training your Border Collie.

9. Preferred Living Conditions

Border Collies should be in an extremely interactive environment in which they have been assigned a clear job. The job might be in a suburban setting and include agility and obedience training. This dog makes an excellent workout and trail companion.

This dog can't live in an apartment as it needs room to move about. Border Collies are extremely active indoors and outdoors. It can do well in a kennel but will need daily activity. It is not recommended to chain the dog up in your backyard all day long.

Chapter 5: Temperament of a Border Collie

Since the Border Collie is fully aware of its surroundings and possesses a high level of intelligence, you will be able to train it effectively. These dogs do really well in different competitions as they excel in sheepdog trails, obedience and agility skills.

It is normal for Border Collies to challenge the authority of their owner in their adolescent stage. The level of dominance can vary significantly in the Border Collies, even when they are in the same litter.

It is essential for the owner to be firm, consistent and a confident leader or the dog might try to take over. If this happens and there hasn't been enough physical and mental exercise and socialization then the dog will become sound sensitive and highly reactive. This will make him a poor pet choice, especially for the families with babies and young children.

This breed has a natural will to please and is a perfectionist. Its main aim is to serve its owner day and night. A Border Collie isn't a pet for those individuals who can't spend much time with their dog as these dogs are not meant to just lie down all day doing absolutely nothing.

If you don't have the time and will to spend a vast amount of your day to train and spend time with your dog then it is better not to adopt a Border Collie and opt for another breed. There are many other breeds that are similar to Border Collies but aren't as demanding as them.

1. Behavior With Children

The Border Collie has the tendency to herd children and even occasionally giving them a nip to the ankle or rear end. This might seem and appear funny at first but it can gradually create a problem, especially if the dog is trained solely to herd livestock.

If you keep letting them herd children, the dog will believe that it is their job and might become aggressive if the children resist. It might even scare the children as the dog takes its job seriously.

It all comes down to how you train your dog. It is important that you immediately stop your dog if it tries to herd children. This might seem like a fun game but the dog will get trained this way and it will be difficult for the owner to put a stop to this habit.

If the training has been done correctly, the Border Collies are perfect with babies and children. They are loving and protective towards them. They will have a thrilling time playing Frisbee or some ball games with the children. It is best to involve your children in training the Border Collie as it teaches the dog who is in charge. With proper training, a Border Collie can become an excellent family pet.

2. Behavior With Other Pets

Early exposure and socialization is essential otherwise Border Collies tend to become shy. If this isn't handled properly, they become reserved around strangers and other pets and may even become aggressive towards them. Since herding is in their blood, they are bound to try to herd other animals.

If they are provided with enough physical and mental activity, these dogs can happily go along with other animals. Sometimes, they can become a little aggressive towards same sex dogs if proper leadership isn't shown to them by the owner.

It is best to keep them away from tiny non-canine pets. However, there are many Border Collies that happily live with other animals, even cats. The important thing is proper training and early socialization.

3. Is the Border Collie An Escape Artist?

Most of the Border Collies are escape artists. With these dogs, it is essential to keep the fences high and wired. The wire must be sunk in the ground along the line of the fence in order to prevent the dogs from digging.

All the doors must be extra secured, as these dogs are smart enough to open the doors. They can open latches and even unlock certain doors to escape.

This breed is extremely agile and can easily climb or jump a 6 foot fence if they really think that they can find something interesting outside. They are extremely good chewers and diggers, this means that if they can't jump a fence they can chew on it or dig to get out.

Chapter 6: Pros and Cons Of Border Collies

Now comes the part where we analyze this dog for what it isn't and what it is. It is important to understand everything about a Border Collie before you make the decision to buy or adopt it as this can save you from a future heartbreak or other damages.

Adopting a dog isn't just a time-oriented task, but also, if you go through with it, then you are in it for a lifetime. This is the reason why it is essential to make the decision wisely after considering all the pros and cons. Here are the advantages and some drawbacks of adopting a Border Collie:

1. The Pros of Border Collies

There are numerous advantages of owning a Border Collie. Here are a few highlights:

- First things first, Border Collies are extremely intelligent. This is a well known fact that this breed is the most intelligent breed of dogs there is. Its intelligent makes it a lot easy to train them. Won't it be great to own the world's most intelligent dog?

- They are quite protective. Border Collies can quickly sense if there is something wrong and their protective mode turns on automatically. Your dog will stand near you and guard you, its ears perked up at the slightest of sounds.

- Another great thing about a Border Collie is that they are very loyal and always eager to please their owner. They will protect you like a guard dog and will give you a loving welcome when they see you after several hours to show you how much you were missed.

- Border Collies are active and are also work oriented. Herding is in their nature and their energy and willingness to do a job makes them perfect as work partners. These dogs love playing and jumping. They also love running in circles as they are herding dogs and love herding people.

- This breed is really friendly. They generally behave really well with other people and other animals, if they are trained properly.

2. The Cons of Border Collies

Border Collies can be all fun and games, and might seem like the perfect companion for you. Undoubtedly, it is one of the best dog breeds there is. However, there are a few drawbacks of owning a Border Collie:

- Firstly, these dogs need wide spaces to run around in. This means that they can't live in apartments or small spaces. Border Collies are energized and pumped up all the time, it is essential for them to run about, herd or do certain jobs so that they energy is utilized properly.

So, if you are living in an apartment or don't have enough space, then it is best to consider another breed. If you do try to contain a Border Collie in small spaces, the result won't be pretty as this dog will try to run about even in that little space and cause damage to your home.

- These dogs need constant mental and physical stimulation to keep them happy. If you don't have enough time to give this dog more than a few hours every day, then it is best to avoid adopting this breed.

They need proper exercise. They have the tendency to become destructive. Border Collies need proper training and physical exercise every day.

- Their herding gene is, on one hand, beneficial; but can become a disadvantage as well. They have a natural tendency to herd; this means they will try to herd other animals and even children.

This habit can be eliminated if they are trained from the start. However, if this habit is not tended to, early on, then it can intensify. Your dog will become aggressive if the children and animals can't be herded properly.

- There is no way you can leave a Border Collie alone for too long. As they are really smart, they can think up ways to exploring things and places which they shouldn't. Thus, they can easily get themselves into trouble.

They can chew and claw at anything that interests them, which can cause damage to your property. An easy solution for this is to hire dog sitters or ask friends and family to help out when you will be away for a longer period of time. You can also opt for a dog day care.

- Border Collies are extremely good escape artists. They can jump through fences or dig underneath them to gain their freedom. They are smart enough to open latches and door knobs. If they feel they are being held captive, they will do whatever they can to escape.

There you have it; all the traits of a Border Collie are now known to you. It is also best to assess a dog's personality and determine if you will be able to handle its responsibility and most importantly, if it will be happy living with you.

Chapter 7: The Selection Process

You now know everything there is to know about a Border Collie's temperament and personality. You are now ready to make a decision about whether you should adopt this dog or not.

If you believe that a Border Collie is perfect for you, then you will want to move on to the next step. Where to buy/adopt a Border Collie? Which one to pick? How to register? Don't worry; this book explains everything you will want to know.

It starts with finding a good breeder. If you make efforts to find the best breeder that you can get, then rest assured that your Border Collie will be well-behaved and healthy. Cross breeding has resulted in polluting this dogs gene and has also enhanced the risk of genetic diseases.

In many cases, breeders try mating their specimen so many times that the litter ends up becoming prone to countless problems that range from chronic health problems to physical deformities. If the mother isn't being properly cared for and is being forced to mate and litter, then it is undoubtedly going to affect her negatively. These negative effects will get transferred to the litter and the owners will have to face the problems.

So, your best bet is to start looking for a good breeder. It is better to travel to another city if you find a genuine breeder there, than to adopt from a local breeder who isn't good enough. This will only lead to problems for you in the future.

Here is some useful information that you will need, to adopt or purchase your Border Collie companion:

1. Where to Purchase Border Collies in the US?

There are several options available to you when it comes to making a decision regarding the purchase of a Border Collie. You can opt for pet shops, puppy farms, professional breeders or private breeders. Every medium has its own advantages and drawbacks. If you aren't short on time or really want to make a great investment, your best chances are with a professional breeder.

In the US, purchasing or adopting a Border Collie while making sure that it is a right breed, is quite easy. This is attributed to the fact that Border Collies are recognized by the American Kennel Club (AKC).

To make sure that you are getting the right dog and the right deal, you just have to ask the breeder about the AKC papers.

AKC is the most trustworthy dog club around the globe. It uses registrations in order to safeguard pedigree breeds. This club was built with the sole aim to protect the sanctity of the gene pool of dogs.

AKC is undoubtedly doing a wonderful job and staying true to its mission for many years. You will be able to get connected to reputed breeders through the American Kennel Club, even in your vicinity. Their website has a detailed breeder database that can enable you to find a reputed breeder, nearest to your area. This will make sure that the dog you purchase is healthy and well-behaved.

If you prefer to look for breeders on your own, make sure that you ask them for AKC papers. Remember that the American Kennel Club registers only pedigree breeds. Their document is ample evidence that the breeder is genuine.

If you are opting for online sellers and breeders, then you must be more careful. Conduct proper research to check the validity of your breeder as it's extremely easy to fool people online. Don't let yourself become a victim. Be sure to not make any money transfers before you have actually seen the dog and its habitat.

2. Where to Purchase Border Collies in the UK?

Although the American Kennel Club is operating in the US and is recognized in many places, its registrations and papers might not work well in the UK. Instead, there is another equivalent dog organization known as The Kennel Club.

Just like the American Kennel Club, UK's The Kennel Club also recognizes the Border Collie as a unique breed. The best thing about the Kennel Club is that it also registers the mixed breeds. So, through this organization, you will be able to attain complete information regarding the orientation of Border Collies and determine whether it is a pure breed or not.

Similar to the US, you will be able to find numerous private breeders, dog shops, professional breeders and puppy farms in the UK from where you can adopt or purchase a Border Collie.

If you also want to play an important role in protecting the gene pool of dogs, then it is best to discourage unethical habits of breeding. This is why it is best to opt for professional breeders. It is also recommended to ask the breeder you select for affiliation records with reputed dog organizations, like the Kennel Club. This will make sure that the breeder you have selected follows the recommended guidelines completely.

Again, if you are opting for online breeders, ensure that you take enough time to determine whether they are authentic or not. Remember, the majority of the genuine breeders won't resort to online selling.

If they do, then they won't mind answering your queries and showing authentication documentations. So, try to dedicate more time to making sure that the online breeder isn't a fraud, because once you have transferred the money to them online, it won't be easy to get it back.

3. Estimated Price for a Border Collie

Another essential factor to consider when moving forward to buy your Border Collie; is performing a market search to determine the estimated cost of the dog. Each dog breed has a different cost. Therefore, it is best to search around and determine the best price that fits your lifestyle.

In the United States, a Border Collie puppy will cost between $300(£205.05) to $800(£546.8). It can cost about $1,000(£683.5) - $1,500(£1025.25) if it is a breeding or show quality dog. The price is usually highly dependent upon the motives of the breeder, the type of puppy care being offered and the puppy's age. If the pup has been already trained, it will increase the price of the Border Collie.

Bear in mind that the price of your puppy won't largely be dependent on the breed or health of the dog. Some genuine breeders might give you a puppy in extremely low costs if they believe that you are truly enthusiastic about the dog. The main motive of genuine breeders is to provide the right home for the dogs instead of simply gaining money from them.

As for the individuals seeking Border Collies in the UK, they might find them a little more expensive as compared to the prices in the US. The prices may be between from £300 to £1,600. Then again, the cost also depends on the breeder.

If the main aim of the breeder is putting the dogs in good homes, then you might get a low price. Furthermore, if the breed isn't pure, then the price will be low as well. Unprofessionally bred or mixed breeds are usually sold at cheaper prices, as the main purpose of the breeder is to have them all adopted as soon as possible.

It is best to take your time in finding the right breeder as the rest of it will fit into place automatically.

4. Signs of a Healthy Border Collie

The association with your pet is hardly for a short duration. When you are heading off to get a Border Collie, be prepared that this relationship is going to be a decade long and will have its fair share of memories and troubles. This is generally linked with the health of your Border Collie; the healthier it is, the longer it will live.

The mission for a healthy pet starts from the time you purchase it. If your Border Collie is facing any health issues in the beginning, then they are probably going to be aggravated throughout its life.

Whilst a genuine breeder and a veterinary doctor will be able to diagnose any health problems beforehand, it is usually quite difficult for an owner, especially a new owner, to diagnose the problem themselves. Therefore, it is recommended to book an appointment with a veterinary doctor so that you can have your Border Collie evaluated medically before you take it home.

In spite of all this, there are a few factors that you should consider and keep in mind before you purchase your Border Collie and make sure that it is healthy.

Records

Always ask the breeder to provide you with the health records of the Border Collie you are about to adopt. This should include all the details about its health; like vaccinations, diseases it has encountered and other trips to the veterinary doctor that the dog has had to make.

It is also best to ask the breeder to give you the 'all clear' certificate that is provided by the veterinary doctor before you make the final payment. This increases the credibility of the breeder. However, in case you aren't provided with the records, ensure that you contact the veterinary doctor to give you the health status of the dog.

Just like other breeds, the Border Collie you get, has to be vaccinated against common dog diseases. It is best to consult the veterinary doctor regarding how many and how frequently your Border Collie will need vaccination and other shots, as it is different with every breed.

If the dog gets too many vaccinations, then it can lead to negative effects. It has been noted in many cases, where a dog has been vaccinated too often, that it has created health complications for the dogs.

If not properly handled, then those too frequent vaccinations can compromise the health and wellbeing of your Border Collie. Therefore, it is highly recommended that you ask the veterinary doctor to make a vaccination schedule for your dog.

It is best to give your dog one vaccination at a time. Also, note how your puppy reacts to it, if it reacts badly to a vaccine, then it is better to steer clear of it. Typically, the vaccinations are injected more frequently in the initial days of the pup's life, as compared to when your dog becomes an adult.

Your Border Collie will have to be vaccinated against distemper, hepatitis, leptospirosis, parovirus and parainfluenza. Initially, it is recommended to take the Border Collie to the vet monthly for the first four months. After that; the shots frequency will be decreased to every six months or once a year.

Always consult the vet to determine the methods of ensuring that the vaccinations are properly dealt with, by the Border Collie. In case of even a slight disturbance, immediately take your dog to the vet to combat the negative reactions immediately.

Any form of negligence can even lead to the death of a pet. Therefore, it is extremely important to take extra precautions and care regarding the health of the dog.

Some Physical Indicators

Before you make the purchase, there are various signs of good health that you can look out for when you make the selection. Here are a few signs to look for in order to get a happy and healthy puppy:

- **Breathing** – a healthy Border Collie will easily and quietly breathe. There won't be any sneezing or coughing, nor will there any signs crusting or discharge around their nostrils.
- **Body** – a healthy Border Collie will look well fed and round. There will be an obvious fat layer around their rib cage.
- **Coat** – the coat of a healthy dog will be soft with no trace of bald spots, greasiness, dullness or dandruff.
- **Energy** – a healthy Border Collie will be energetic and alert. If is seems lazy and sluggish, then there is bound to be a health problem.
- **Hearing** – clap your hands behind the dog's head. If it is a healthy dog then it will react immediately.
- **Genitals** – there won't be any visible discharge around or in the anal or genital region of a healthy Border Collie.
- **Mobility** – a healthy Border Collie will run and walk normally without limping, wobbling or seeming sore, stiff or weak.
- **Vision** – a healthy Border Collie will have clear and bright eyes without any discharge or crust. They will be able to notice a ball rolling past them if it is within their vision field.

If the Border Collie you have selected faces even the slightest bit of difficulties in any of the above mentioned aspects, then get a veterinary doctor to do an inspection before you sign the contract with the breeder.

5. *Factors To Consider Before Making The Final Decision*

There are numerous more important factors that must be considered while you purchase your Border Collie. Here are some of the most significant ones to help you in making your final decision:

How Many

How many Border Collie dogs do you want to adopt or purchase? Given their active and intelligent nature, you might get inclined to get multiple ones. Who wouldn't want to be surrounded by such incredibly smart, active and protective dogs? But this might be a really difficult decision to make.

If you already have experience of handling Border Collie dogs, then by all means buy more than one dog. However, if you have never had any experience of handling this breed, then it is recommended to avoid getting multiple dogs, as Border Collies can be a handful.

If one Border Collie can give you enough trouble, imagine what it will be like to handle two or three of them at once! It is best to get experience with this breed first and once you have raised a well-behaved loving dog, you can always get one or two more.

If you are confident about your decision of getting multiple Border Collies, then go ahead. If you work hard in training them well; then you will end up with extremely loving and amazing companions for life.

However, beware of competition. Border Collies don't like getting ignored because of other dogs, even of the same breed. For this reason, getting multiple Border Collies at once is a far better idea than raising one and then getting another one, as the first one will start feeling neglected.

If you get multiple puppies at once and raise them together, this issue won't surface. Again, make sure that you will be able to handle the responsibility of handling multiple Border Collies.

Gender

Looking at the bigger picture, the gender of the Border Collie doesn't matter. Both female and male Border Collies are equally lovable and affectionate. They are both same sized and have similar looks.

The majority of their mental and physical characteristics will precisely match one another. The one thing that you will have to think of is whether you want your Border Collie to raise a family.

In general, with female Border Collies, the issues of 'mating' and 'coming to heat' might be painful not only for your pet but also for you.

This is the same with the male Border Collies but it is far less daunting as a male dog doesn't have to experience the consequences of mating. Nevertheless, this is a problem that requires preplanning and foresightedness to ensure that there is a contingency plan in place, in case of any problems.

Getting your dog neutered and spayed is one method of resolving this emotional problem. Although, this activity is quite debatable as it will alter the nature of your dog. This act is also considered as a violation of animal rights.

Age

The newborns get their first nutrition from their mothers and they learn their first values from their mothers and littermates. Therefore, it is significant to give the Border Collies enough time with their littermates and mothers so that they attain the basic training before they are separated from them and placed in different homes.

It is strictly recommended not to separate the litter from their parents for the initial two months. The initial eight weeks of a dog's life are extremely important to define its life progress. Those puppies that are separated too early from their mothers and littermates tend to develop personality and temperament disorders as they grow up. They might even develop health problems.

When the puppies become stable after a period of eight weeks, the breeders usually try to encourage them to adapt to the environment. This means gradually replacing the mother's nutrition with pet food, solid food and including liquid food in their diet. This is the time when is best for adoption.

Aside from adopting or purchasing puppies, you can also opt for rescuing Border Collies. These dogs are the ones coming from battered homes or are in a battered state. These dogs can be provided with proper shelter in your home till their natural demise. In most cases, the organizations or breeders rescuing dogs, give them away free of charge for genuine buyers who really care for dogs.

However, this means more issues with the pet. The rescued dogs are more likely to have a number of health issues and might even have personality disorders that can make it a little difficult to tame them.

If you are opting for a rescued dog, then it is recommended that you already have some experience of handling a difficult and troublesome dog.

It is better to remember that in both ages – puppy or adult, the requirements of Border Collies will vary. Ensure that you can care for the dog in the best way possible. This will be the foundation stone towards a happy, healthy and long relationship with your Border Collie.

6. The Registration Process

When you are completely satisfied with the health of your Border Collie, there is one more thing that you must do. You have to register your Border Collie with the American Kennel Club if it is a purebred. This will ensure a generation of purebred dogs whenever you opt to get your pet mated.

Furthermore, such a registration will also enable you to participate in various dog shows that happen regularly throughout the year around the globe. This will give you an opportunity to connect with other dog owners from all over the word and show off your amazing Border Collie!

If you live in the UK, ensure that your dog gets registered with The Kennel Club. As this dog organization registers both mixed breeds and purebreds, there won't be any problems in getting your pet registered.

It is recommended for every dog owner to play their part in eradicating unhealthy breeding practices which can be achieved by registering your dog or adopting or purchasing a registered dog.

Aside from these significant facts that compel you to reconsider having your dog registered with the right dog organization, there are many other advantages as well. For example, if your Border Collie somehow escapes and ends up in a dog pound, then that registration will keep it safe till you go and get back your dog.

Since Border Collies are really good escape artists, this is bound to happen several times. If your dog isn't registered, it will become harder to rescue it in time. If a dog is found by the authorities without a registration, your pet is likely to go to a dog pound or will be put to a never ending sleep if not rescued in time.

A dog registration will also save you from getting penalized unnecessarily and doesn't cost a lot at all.

Be aware that an unregistered dog can cost you a penalty.

The registration process also establishes your ownership over your Border Collie. It becomes emotionally and legally yours. Registration of your dog goes a long way to show how connected you are with your pet.

7. How To Bond With Your Border Collie

There is no magic wand for making your Border Collie love you but getting connected can work wonders for you. Your Border Collie is quite aware of what's going on around and behaves accordingly. Instinct is what Border Collies respond to when they go from calm to mad in seconds. In a hyper state the Border Collie is not open to learning and will not respond to any of your "commands".

On the other hand when Border Collies are in a conscious state of mind they learn, as they're not in an instinctive state. If you desire to activate that magic wand and get connected with your Border Collie, understanding its various emotional states is imperative.

You can make your Border Collie think and respond logically by understanding its emotional states to help it become more aware of its surroundings. However, when it comes to communication with your Border Collie, there are certain ins and outs that you need to know of. Let's quickly take a look at these ins and outs.

Decode Border Collies Body Language

In order to let you know what they are thinking and feeling, Border Collies use body language, as this is what they're good at. Whether your dog is feeling relaxed, stressed out, wanting to play a bit or frightened, you will know all this via the positioning of your Border Collie's tail, ears and head. To help you understand what your Collie is trying to tell you, here are some basic cues.

- Your Collie is happy and wants to play if its tail is wagging, eyes are shining and ears are up.

44

- Your Collie is feeling stressed out, angry and scared if its tail is pointed downwards, lips are wrapped and ears are back. At such times its best to leave the Border Collie alone and not bother it too much.
- Your Border Collie could be worried, exploring a smell or looking for a place to relieve itself if it's sniffing around. At such a time the Collie wants you to stay calm, does not want to be disturbed and is like a dog on a mission.
- Lastly, your Border Collie could be severely stressed out if it's drooling, panting or yawning. There are many reasons for this feeling including weird or significantly high noises, your demeanor, lots of people being around and isolation.

Keeping Your Body Language in check

Your Border Collie will get conflicting messages if the signals your body sends and what you verbally utter out are not in sync. Body language is what the Border Collie uses to understand what you're feeling. Whether you are worried, happy or angry, the Border Collie will know even the slightest shift in behavior.

If your Border Collie is nervous or frightened, you can calm it by showing a good body posture, controlling your breathing and tone of voice and by projecting a calm demeanor. If you're able to do all those things, your Border Collie will get the signal that my owner is calm and has everything under control so there is no need to be nervous. On the other hand, your Collie will become nervous and anxious if you were to demonstrate a similar behavior.

Know your Border Collie's Personality

Fostering a better understanding between yourself and your Border Collie will help you to find out about its personality which in turn will help you get connected better with your Border Collie. The Collie is very similar in nature to humans.

If the nature of your Collie is assertive and strong and you're being overly nice with it then it will take advantage of you and assert its will onto you. On the other hand you will frighten your Border Collie if it's timid in nature and you come too strong. Your Collie's learning process can suffer greatly if you misjudge its personality.

There should be no Discrepancy in the learning Process

If you keep changing your rules then the Border Collie won't get them. An unrealistic expectation of your Border Collie would be, expecting it to stay off the couch when it has dirty feet when it's allowed on its every single day of the week.

Even though the Border Collie is an intelligent dog, it isn't intelligent enough to know such discrepancies.

The learning process of dogs is very different from humans as they have a unique communication system. Narrowing the gap between what your Collie actually learns and what you intend it to learn should be your aim.

Dog training becomes so much easier if you're able to do just that. In turn, your Border Collie will become more and more a part of family and friend's activities as its behavior will improve and it will become a well-behaved dog. This will be a win-win situation as both you and the Border Collie will be happy and the perks of this connection will be countless.

Being Patient with your Border Collie

It is important for you to remember that success does not come overnight and success with your over hyped Border Collie will come gradually over time. It may take several months but if you do all the right things, in due time your dog will trust you with everything. As a result, your Border Collie will become relaxed, will start to enjoy himself and will let go of that uncanny feeling for biting. You may even let it participate in dog competitions, as it is a very agile dog.

Getting connected will result in your Border Collie becoming more focused, having better concentration, being less sensitive and will enjoy being touched. Above all you and your Border Collie will become a team and you will be amazed by the joy that brings you.

Chapter 8: Puppy Proofing Your Place

The arrival of your new companion may just be a few days away if you have done half of your work by short listing your Border Collie and are halfway done with the ownership transfer and the payment. This may well be an experience that excites you but being prepared to accommodate the new addition to your house is extremely essential.

Deciding upon the sleeping place for your pet, his food and daily activities etc. are things you need to be done with before making a move for the Border Collie. If you don't want to be hit on the head in the near future by these things, it is best you start planning for them if you haven't already.

Waiting to deal with these things after your four-legged friend enters the house is a big mistake on your part. The reason being you won't have much time to get things in order as the Border Collie will take up most of your time.

The first two weeks after purchasing the Collie will be a handful for you and you won't get much time to sort out things. You will be at a disadvantage if you don't put your act together in good time. In order for you to assist your pet through its initial transitional phase, here are the basic necessities you need to fulfill. Not fulfilling them can spell disaster for you.

1. Changes You Need To Make To Your Home

If you want to make sure that your house is a good fit for your Border Collie, you'll need to make a few alterations to it. Your pet's well being and your best interests depend upon it.

The importance of the furniture around your house is not something your pets recognize thus it is highly likely that puppies will nibble (especially when they are teething) and flex their claws at these things. If you want to protect your property and puppy, here are the things you need to do.

Fencing your house

Border Collies have an inclination to dig in to find their way, thus building a well rooted fence around your home is the need of the hour. Having this contingency in place before your puppy tries to make the escape is in your best interests even though the puppy won't be trying it all the time.

Have Latches Everywhere

All the places, like cabinets and cupboards in the kitchen, used to stock toxic chemicals like cleaners etc, need to have latches if you want to avoid your Border Collie experimenting with them. To enable doors to close on their own you may want to install devices on them. Your Border Collie should not have access to personal rooms, nurseries and similar places. The consequences can be alarming if your pet chokes on your child's toy or any other product with similar characteristics. You need to lock up all cleaning products, chemicals and medicines to keep them out of your pet's sight.

Keep them away from wires

It's not a big deal if you leave a wire or two lying haphazardly on the ground under normal circumstances but if you have a pet in the house it can be consequential. Dogs have an inquisitive nature and this is the reason an unsheathed wire may catch their attention. They might use their claws to play with these exposed wires which may result in an electric shock. Have these wires placed in the corners of the room so that they are away from the Border Collie. To prevent scratches use protective covering made from durable plastic. Also to make sure the wires don't catch their attention, give them something else to keep them busy.

Keep all fragile and potentially dangerous items out of your Pet's sight

Things that shatter on impact including crystal, glass or other similar material should be kept out of your pet's sights. Also,

49

things that have the tendency to be lethal like remotes, kitchen utensils, containers, sharp-edged items, plastic bags, CDs, DVDs and keys should be stocked behind closed doors. Care for your pet just like you would your child as it does not realize and recognize any danger that may lie ahead.

Have a Door for your Border Collie

In order to ensure that you Border Collie moves easily in and out of the house install a pet door on your main door. The size of the door needs to be appropriate so that your Border Collie does not feel strangled and has no obstructions.

If you do not install a pet door don't be surprised when you notice claw marks on your door as it may want to go out to play or attend to nature's call but has no idea how to make it possible.

Not installing a pet door is a loss-loss situation as both you and the Collie suffer, so make sure you install one.

Make your washroom Dog-Proof

It is important that you have your washroom door locked at all times. You may use an automatic lock door if you deem it necessary for keeping your pet out. An attractive and equally hazardous place for your Border Collie is the flush bowl. Also the slippery floors pose a threat to your dog's safety. If you want to make sure your pet stays away from your washroom, keep it locked. Make sure you do not leave your pet unattended until it becomes completely potty trained.

Keep certain objects and edibles out of your pet's reach

Don't leave your chocolate wrappers lying around as most Border Collies do not tolerate chocolates well. You need to make arrangements to keep your pet away from plants if it has any allergy to the plant. You can do this either by making the place of the plant a no go area for your pet or placing the plant in a place where the pet cannot reach.

Use barriers

Whether it is indoors or outdoors, use barriers wherever required. Use a barrier such as a grill to protect your cabinets and sofas. Also, do not leave your dog unattended in the garden if you wish to maintain its look. For your own good, use barriers in front of pools and every other object you don't want your pet to sniff around.

2. Preliminary Shopping List

Be fully prepared to receive your pet in a travel crate – it is the best that will be arranged by most breeders. As the pet is new and possibly bewildered, it is best not to carry it in your arms. Besides this vital necessity (to make transportation possible), there are a dozen other things you will need to purchase so that your pet can survive a minimum of two weeks in the new home.

If you are planning to take your new pet shopping even before it has settled, rest assured it is a sure recipe for disaster. Have enough stocks to last you two weeks before you bring the new one home. By this time, your pet will have adjusted to the new owner, new rules and new lifestyle. Hence it will pose fewer challenges while handling.

Here is a list of things you need to purchase – before the new one walks in!

Visiting the veterinary

Call in to book your appointment if needed. It is like a gift from you to your dog – something that it will definitely be thankful for even if it is not able to say it out loud. Have it vaccinated for all major diseases and draft up a schedule for regular checkups. Mark it on your calendar so you don't miss out on it.

Remember, your vet can see beyond the furry shiny coat and hence is in a better state to identify any imminent health problems and diseases.

As in the case of breeder, take your time in locating a certified and genuine veterinary doctor.

Pet Food

This includes food, treats and all other form of edibles for your pet.
This is one thing you will need within 24 hours of getting the dog home. Moreover, this is one thing that is directly related to its health, rationality, irritability and resistance.
Try to get the same stocks of pet food your Border Collie is already accustomed to at the breeder's – so it can feel at home. Be foresighted and get enough food to last you a minimum of two weeks.

Food and Water bowls

As much as you would like it, your canine friends cannot feast with you using your kitchen utensils. They need to have their own bowls for food and water.

Make sure you have purchased these beforehand to minimize the stress of finding an alternative impromptu when the need arises. Also, keep in mind that your pet associates these bowls with nutrition and will continue to do so for a long time. So it is a good idea to invest in high-quality and durable bowls.
Have a good look at the breeder's options before making your decision so that your new friend does not feel like a stranger.

ID tags, collars and leash

These accessories mark your dog and establish your ownership for the world to see.
It is also imperative for you to get these affairs in order well before you get your new companion home. Feeling as a captive being taken away from home, your new pet is likely to make a dash into the unknown whenever it is given the opportunity.

Also, in a foreign neighborhood, chances of it finding its way to your home are next to impossible. So make sure your new friend is fastened adequately to your vehicle to prevent such unfortunate incidences.

Even if it does, the identification documents around its neck will prove to be a life saver – someone else who comes across your dog will be able to return it home if your dog carries its home address! Keep the Border Collie's dog's size, strength and personality traits in mind while shopping for its identification accessories.

Dog bed

After a long day of getting accustomed to foreign practices and obeying orders from a relatively unknown master, your dog needs adequate rest so that it wakes up fresh and healthy the next morning. A dog bed lined with soft linens and soft cushions work well. If your pet does not sleep well, it will eventually lead it towards bigger health problems.

So make sure you place its bed in a secluded and silent corner of the house. Also, help your pet associate this space with "night" and "sleep" so it is easier to command it to rest.
Rest assured this is not something you can leave on for later – your canine friend needs a good night's sleep every night!

Dog toys

Dogs don't sleep well with a whole lot of built up energy in their bodies. Assuming you don't have the time or the will to walk your pet every evening/morning in the first few days of association; dog toys are the second best alternative to achieve this motive. It helps in keeping your pet occupied and entertained (without your active effort). Moreover, dog toys are also an effective way of stimulating the dog's brain and helping it develop its mental capacities. Use intelligent dog toys and obstacles to help your canine friend develop intellectually and physically – as it would if it were to live in the wild!

Travel crate

You won't need it immediately (unless your breeder fails to offer the initial carry crate) but you eventually will. Imagine the first time you go out shopping after your new pet makes it home. How do you imagine you will carry the fragile being? Carrying it in your arms, though an impressive gesture, will not work well as your pet will feel threatened by the sudden presence of hundreds of other shoppers.

On top of this, there are other places you might need to go to – office, veterinary doctor, your own doctor and others – that will definitely not accommodate an open dog. So it is better to purchase a travel crate well beforehand to keep away from embarrassments.

Dog clothes

This becomes exceptionally imperative if you are planning to purchase your Border Collie companion during the winter. Also, do remember to buy a few warm clothes for your dog if you plan to keep it outdoors – even in the summer. The cold can get to its skin and make it ill before you would realize what has happened. Keep your defenses up to protect your pet against all odds.

Grooming supplies

Dogs are inquisitive creatures. They have inexplicable interest in finding out what is hidden in the darkest of corners. They can easily be led to places by the smallest of insects. So naturally, they don't last a week without getting dirty. You will need to groom your Border Collie on a daily basis to keep its coat smooth and tangle-free.

Having grooming supplies beforehand is a good idea. Imagine having to go to the supermarket with an unkempt dog that clearly says its master does not care!
Be foresighted enough to prepare for things that are expected to happen. Make sure you search through all alternatives on the

market before settling for a few – it helps you get the best possible items!

Also, make sure you have ample supplies to last two weeks. It would typically include a shampoo, scrub, dental hygiene solutions, nail clippers, hair tonic, conditioners, and everything else that you would like to use for your new pet's beauty! The sky is the limit!

Even so, it is recommended not to use a lot of chemicals on your pet, as an excess of everything is detrimental!

Puppy pads

No one likes to witness a trail of unsightly liquids or solids winded all across the house. The odor makes it even more unbearable. Do yourself a favor and use puppy pads for the first few days – especially if your canine friend is not yet potty trained.

Train it to use the open outdoors for relieving itself. It will become possible and tolerable over-time!

Once you are out on the shopping spree, you will come across a number of other items that are not on this list but might apparently look useful. Evaluate its utility in the light of your pet before making your purchase. However, if it seems like an absolute necessity, it is better not to let it be left for a later date.

Admittedly, these accessories summed up with the cost of acquiring a pet (payment to the breeder, registrations etc) can amount to a significant portion of your savings. So you need to be mentally prepared for this kind of expenditure.

It is expected to be an association of a decade or two; so rest assured it will be an ongoing expense rather than just a one-time incident!

Also, keep in mind that most of the items on your shopping list will last quite a few years before they become unusable, broken or "too small" for use (provided you make intelligent decisions in the first place!). So usually the returns on your investment are quite appreciable if you are looking long term.

Having a new companion inevitably calls for a few adjustments. You will need to make quite a few sacrifices to let your new friend settle in. But it will be worth the time and effort!

Chapter 9: Common Health Problems

I will talk more about medical concerns later in this book; the Border Collie in general is a fairly healthy breed. As it has been bred to be highly athletic and strong, the Border Collie is a fairly healthy dog. As a result of early farmer's intensive screening, Border Collie's have strong respiratory and circulatory systems.

However, just as in the case of any other dogs, the Border Collie is prone to some health problems. A health issue that the Border Collie develops from birth is a congenital skeletal problem which is also common for a few other medium to large sized dogs.

A few health problems get genetically transferred into a Border Collie. Hip dysplasia is one of these genetically transferred health issues. However this issue is not life threatening. Other diseases include Neuronal Ceroid lipofuscinosis, Collie Eye Anomaly and Trapped Neutrophil Syndrome.

The Border Collie can turn out to be a great companion and pet for you, provided you've carried out an early diagnosis and treat this health condition.

1. Common Symptoms and Diseases

A multi factorial disease, dysplasia develops as a result of a defect in the hip and hip joint. Basically, dysplasia is decaying of these body parts. Even though this problem gets genetically transferred into the Border Collie, environmental factors such as nutrition or behavior play a role as well.

If the diet of the Border Collie is one that promotes quick growth and the pups are accommodated on slippery floors then the chances of dysplasia developing increases. This means that taking care of their diet is important.

In order to ensure a balanced growth of soft muscles and bones, there needs to be a perfect balance of minerals and vitamins in the diet. Also, activities such as climbing stairs, slips and jumping must be avoided by the dog as it may cause health problems for the pup.

It is important that you monitor and control your young companion. While it's natural for your little friend to climb up and down, run and jump, too much of these activities can be harmful for the Collie's health. Therefore these activities must be controlled.

The hip joints of a Border Collie suffering from dysplasia are badly developed. The head of the hip joint is unable to fit properly into the hip.

This results in the hip becoming unbalanced and becomes a carrier of pain, weakness and inflammation.

The health issues the Border Collie is suffering from may not become transparent until they are in the advanced stage. This causes the symptoms to often be misleading. The symptoms may range anywhere between small irregularities in movement to severe physical impairment.

The existence of the disease may be indicated by these symptoms but the only true way to find out about it is through a diagnosis.

2. Early Diagnosis

Radiology is probably the best method to see if the dog is prone to disease or not as there is no genetic method available for it. However, you'll get puppies free of dysplasia if you bring together dogs with good hips to copulate.

In order to get the best DNA reports, the diagnosis should be carried out under general anesthesia and should be carried out by a veterinarian. The diagnosis will help establish the severity of the dysplasia. Therefore indicating which dogs are not suitable for breeding purposes and the best suited rehabilitation program.

Asking the owners of the puppy's parents may be a good way to get informed about the potential health risks the Border Collie may be prone to. You can prevent some serious future health problems by asking the previous owners and devising appropriate measures.

3. Shots, Vaccinations and Regular Check-Ups

Your pet – irrespective of which species or breed it is – will need to be vaccinated against a wide range of diseases. This is done to ensure longevity and better immune system development for your pet.

An infectious killer, parvovirus is a fatal disease that your border Collie can pick up. In order to ensure that you avoid such a scenario and prevent this disease from developing, get your Border Collie regularly vaccinated.

Make sure you keep your puppy's vaccinations current and get your vet's advice if you want to avoid the heartbreak of seeing your dog develop a wearing disease.

Discuss in detail with your veterinary doctor about how to take care of your Border Collie. Also, express your concerns over the vaccination schedule if any. Make sure you and your veterinary doctor are on the same page with respect to the Border Collie.

Don't forget to take your pet in for regular check-ups. Once your pet is through with its initial vaccinations and shots, make sure you are still paying a visit to the veterinary doctor every month or two. This will help your vet diagnose problems in the early stages and treat them accordingly.

Your Border Collie needs to be vaccinated every month for the first four months of its life. Then on, the frequency is reduced to once a year. Make sure you are not missing out on these appointments. Your pet's health and well being is your responsibility, so make sure you are proving to be the right owner for your canine companion!

Chapter 10: Caring for Your Border Collie

So far you've been exposed to the idea of getting a Border Collie dog, purchasing and bringing it home, keeping it healthy and being a responsible owner. However, this is where the real challenge begins. This sections talks about how you will be required to care for your Border Collie dog – from the very basics to the advanced maintenance regimes. Read through this section carefully to understand how best to care for your puppy.

1. The First Few Days and Weeks

Before bringing your new companion home, make sure you've put the right barriers in place. Sweep the floors carefully to eliminate all sources of discomfort for the puppy. Also, close the doors to your personal rooms. Your puppy does not need to have access to all rooms of the house. Just keep one or two doors open to the rooms that have been puppy-proofed.

Also, make sure you have at least two weeks' puppy supplies readily available with you. Unless you have support at home, you won't be leaving the premises for shopping before the second week. So it is best to have your act in order before the little one walks in.

For the first few weeks, you will have to let your Border Collie get accustomed to the "foreign" environment of your house. It will explore the territories and try to understand what is being expected of it in the given scenario.

It is important for you to be consistent with your puppy's routine – its sleep time, its feeding time, its exercise time and so on and so forth. Inconsistency will give rise to personality disorders and irritability which, in the long run, will impact you negatively!

The first few weeks are ideal for potty training; so invest in your efforts wisely. Let your puppy know where it can relieve itself and where it is considered inappropriate. Kennel training should also be conducted to establish your supremacy over your pet. The first few days and weeks are critical to the long term relationship with your pet – make sure you are investing in its grooming wisely!

Also, never leave your puppy out of supervision. If your puppy is allowed to have its way, it will most surely opt for disaster – for itself as well as for you. Keep a close eye on its activities and curb any evil intentions in the bud. This is important for a healthy relationship later on.

Last but not the least; stay strict but loving with your pet. It needs to know who the boss is but also needs to understand that it is being loved. Don't make it feel too neglected or troubled – it will try to make a run for it. If it is being pampered too much, it will begin considering itself as the "leader". Establish a balance so the relationship can be carried forth ideally!

2. Setting the Rules

First and foremost, before you begin training your pet, you need to lay out a few rules in a language that it understands. It may be rules like where to relieve, what to do for play, the rooms which are out of bounds for it and others. You will also need to establish certain hand gestures or words associated with specific actions or meanings.

The first and foremost rule that you need to set is to establish your supremacy over your pet. It needs to understand that you are the only leader in the house. Even with the dominant nature of dogs, your pet needs to understand and register your control.

It needs to be subservient to you. It needs to understand that it is in no position to challenge its master. And integration of this value begins when you bring the puppy home.

Never let your puppy lead you into the house. It should always be the one following you around the house. Make sure all human beings are entering the house before the puppy – it tells the dog where it stands in the hierarchy. Border Collie's are inherently hyper dogs with destructive behaviors.

However, if you are looking for a well behaved puppy, you will need to harden yourself and deal with this natural instinct of the Collie. All dogs essentially have the same nature – they need to be treated alike in order to keep them disciplined.

Besides this, keep the no-puppy zones in your house locked at all times. If you see your puppy trying to break in, let it know this behavior is undesirable. Penalize it if necessary – it will not try to transgress limits once it understands.

Let your puppy know where it is supposed to sleep, eat or drink. Also, build a schedule for its activities – when it is supposed to feast or sleep. Administer these values so the Border Collie is less challenging when it matures.

3. Grooming Concerns

The first thing any one sees about your pet is how well it is kept. They don't groom themselves; you need to be making an active effort to keep your Border Collie presentable at all times. Here are a few grooming tips that you need to be careful about.

Its Coat

The Border Collie has two main types of coats. One coat is hair that can grow up to 3 inches long while the other is fairly short and shiny. The hair will become greasy and tangled if it's not taken care of. Therefore, regular brushing is required for the coat, especially if it's the longer type.

In the shedding seasons you need to be extra careful when brushing your border Collie. Unless it absolutely necessary; do not dry shampoo or bathe your Border Collie. The Border Collie's coat will be stripped of nutrients leaving it fragile and dry if you wash it more than its requirement. Also, washing your border Collie with a specific shampoo design is important.

Its Nails

Allowing your Border Collie to have long, untrimmed nails can result in various health hazards including infections or an irregular and uncomfortable gait that can result in damage to their skeleton.

Although most dogs do not particular enjoy the process of having their nails trimmed, and most humans find the exercise to be a little scary, regular nail trimming is a very important grooming practice that should never be overlooked. In order to keep your adult Border Collie dog's toenails in good condition and the proper length, you will need to purchase a plier type nail trimmer at a pet store and learn how to correctly use it.

When your Border Collie is a small puppy, it will be best to trim their nails with a pair of nail scissors, which you can purchase at any pet store, that are smaller and easier to use on puppy nails. All you need to do is snip off the curved tip of each nail.

Further, if you want your dog's nails to be smooth, without the sharp edges clipping alone can create, you will also want to invest in a toenail file or a special, slow speed, rotary Dremel™ trimmer, equipped with a sanding disk, which is designed especially for dog nails.

Some dogs will prefer the rotary trimmer to the squeezing sensation of the nail clipper and when you keep your dog's nails regularly trimmed, the Dremel™ may be the only tool you will ever need.

Dental Hygiene

Yes, your dog needs regular brushing as well. Bad breath and inadequate dental hygiene can eventually lead to bigger problems – including upset stomach and halitosis. Make sure you brush your pet's teeth every day (or every few days)!

You can use commercially produced products or use homemade ones by combining baking soda with water. Use soft nylon cloth or commercial toothbrushes to clean its teeth. Don't agitate your pet, as its teeth are the last place you want to be near to while it is angry! Inability to do so can lead your Border Collie dog towards gum diseases that can aggravate into teeth-loss. Keep your dog's smile healthy – brush its teeth and gums regularly.

Have its teeth and gums regularly inspected by the veterinary doctor. This will help in diagnosing a problem at the earliest. Consequently, it will be easier to devise a plan of action to overcome this problem in a timely manner.

Its Ears

Have your Border Collie dog checked regularly for ear infections. Ear cropping does not prevent ear infections. This becomes more important once your Border Collie has had its periodic bath.

You can find a number of chemical solutions on the market to clean your pet's ears. Make sure you've consulted the veterinarian before using any. Also, seek advice from your veterinary doctor to find out how best to clean your canine's ears. Too much debris can build up into a major health problem. Most evidently though, too much debris can lead to loss of hearing, which might be misinterpreted as lack of obedience.

Do yourself and your Border Collie dog a favor; clean its ears regularly so you can nurture a well-rounded relationship with your pet!

Its Eyes

Every dog should have their eyes regularly wiped with a warm, damp cloth to remove build up of daily secretions in the corners of the eyes that can be unattractive and uncomfortable for the dog as the hair becomes glued together.

If this build up is not removed every day, it can quickly become a cause of bacterial yeast growth that can lead to eye infections.

When you take a moment every day to gently wipe your dog's eyes with a warm, moist cloth, you will help to keep your dog's eyes comfortable and infection free.

Bathing

Step One: Before you get your Border Collie anywhere near the water, it's important to make sure that you brush out any debris, or dead hair from their coat before you begin the bathing process.

As well, removing any debris from your dog's coat beforehand will make the entire process easier on you, your dog, and your drains, which will become clogged with dead hair if you don't remove it beforehand.

Step Two: If your Border Collie has a longer coat, the process will be much easier if you first spray the coat with a light mist of leave-in conditioner before brushing. This will also help to protect the hair strands against breakage.

Step Three: Whether you're bathing your Border Collie in your laundry tub, bathtub or sink, you will always want to first lay down a rubber bath mat to provide a more secure footing for your dog and to prevent your tub or sink from being scratched.

Step Four: Have everything you need for the bath (shampoo, conditioner, sponge, towels) right next to the sink or tub, so you don't have to go searching once your dog is already in the water.

Place cotton balls in your Border Collie dog's ear canals to prevent accidental splashes from entering the ear canal that could later cause an ear infection.

Step Five: Fill the tub or sink with four to six inches of lukewarm water (not too hot as dogs are more sensitive to hot water than us humans) and put your Border Collie dog in the water. Completely wet your dog's coat right down to the skin by using a detachable showerhead. If you don't have a spray attachment, a cup or pitcher will work just as well.

Step Six: Apply shampoo as indicated on the bottle instructions by beginning at the head and working your way down the back. Be careful not to get shampoo in the eyes, nose, mouth or ears. Comb the shampoo lather through your dog's hair with your fingers, making sure you don't miss the areas under the legs and tail.

Step Seven: After allowing the shampoo to remain in your dog's coat for a couple of minutes, thoroughly rinse the Border Collie dog's coat, right down to the skin with clean, lukewarm water using the spray attachment, cup or pitcher. Comb through your dog's coat with your fingers to make sure all shampoo residues has been completely rinsed away.

Any shampoo remaining in a dog's coat will lead to irritation and itching. Once you've rinsed, take the time to rinse again, especially in the armpits and underneath the tail area. Use your hands to gently squeeze all excess water from your dog's coat.

Step Eight: Apply conditioner as indicated on the bottle instructions and work the conditioner throughout your dog's coat. Leave the conditioner in your dog's coat for two minutes and then thoroughly rinse again with warm water, unless the conditioner you are using is a *"leave-in"*, no-rinse formula.

The best conditioner for a Border Collie will contain mink oil, which adds a gloss to deepen and enrich the natural color of the coat.

It is also a good idea to choose a brand of conditioner that contains sunscreen to help protect from ultraviolet radiation when your dog is outside on sunny days.

Applying a good conditioner containing protein to your Border Collie's coat after bathing will help to rebuild, restructure and protect the coat by bonding to the shaft of each individual hair.

Pull the plug on your sink or tub and let the water drain away as you use your hands to squeeze excess water from your Border Collie's legs and feet.

Step Nine: Immediately out of the water, wrap your Border Collie in dry towels so they don't get cold and use the towels to gently squeeze out extra water before you allow them to shake and spray water everywhere.

If your dog has longer hair, do not rub their coat with the towels, as this will create tangles and breakage in the longer hair.

Dry your Border Collie right away with your hand held hairdryer and be careful not to let the hot air get too close to their skin.

If your dog's hair is longer, blow the hair in the direction of growth to help prevent breakage and if the hair is short, you can use your hand or a soft brush or comb to lift and fluff the coat to help it dry more quickly.

Place your hand between the hairdryer and your Border Collie's hair so that they will never get a direct blast of hot air and never blow air directly into their face or ears. Don't forget to remove the cotton balls from their ears.

Brushing and Combing

Your Border Collie will have long hairs that are prone to getting tangled unless they are cut short. In order to get the best of everything, you will need to brush its coat on a daily basis – preferably multiple times during the day – to keep it free from tangles.

Use a soft and organic brush to straighten its hair. Also, always brush its hair in one direction making sure it is aligned properly with the direction of growth. Combing the hairs in any other direction will put unnecessary strain on the hair and cause breakage.

Brushing the hair multiple times during the day will ensure there are no unnecessary tangles forming in the canine's coat. Brushing and combing is one way to express your love for your canine and will therefore help in bonding. Make sure you are spending sufficient time at the task.

Also, don't brush the hair on the surface. Make sure you are stimulating the skin as well through the brushing process. This will not only improve the blood circulation towards the hairs and skin but also improve the quality of hair.

The key to grooming your Border Collie is to prevent its hair from tangling into knots. These notorious knots can become a challenge to untangle – in the worst case scenario; you might need to remove the knots by cutting off the hair. Brush regularly and bathe it periodically. If your Border Collie looks presentable, you've done a commendable job of caring for it!

4. Feeding Concerns

The next important thing you need to be aware about is the feeding concerns your pet has. Here is a little insight into the Border Collie's eating patterns.

Feeding Young Border Collie Dogs

For growing puppies, a general feeding rule of thumb is to feed 10% of the puppy's present body weight or between 2% and 3% of their projected adult weight each day.

Keep in mind that high energy puppies will require extra protein to help them grow and develop into healthy adult dogs, especially during their first two years of life.

There are now many foods on the market that are formulated for all stages of a dog's life (including the puppy stage), so whether you choose one of these foods or a food specially formulated for puppies, they will need to be fed smaller meals more frequently throughout the day (3 or 4 times), until they are at least one year of age.

Choose quality sources of meat protein for healthy puppies and dogs, including beef, buffalo, chicken, duck, fish, hare, lamb, ostrich, pork, rabbit, turkey, venison, or any other source of wild meaty protein.

Feeding Adult Border Collie Dogs

An adult dog will generally need to be fed between 2% and 3% of their body weight each day. Read the labels and avoid foods that contain a high amount of grains and other fillers. Choose foods that list high quality meat protein as the main ingredient.

Frequency of Feeding

How frequently you need to feed your dog largely depends on its physical characteristics. For instance, some Border Collie dogs like to consume several small servings during the day, a few eat well in the evening while a few might work well with a twice-a-day regime. By and large, you will need to contemplate the type of Border Collie you've ended up with.

Ideally, during the early months, it is recommended to feed your Border Collie multiple servings during the day – about four small servings throughout the day. Once your Border Collie hits the six-month mark, you can try reducing the frequency to thrice or twice per day.

Keep in mind that your Border Collie should not have the liberty to feed as and when it wills. Designate a specific time frame in which the Border Collie is allowed to feast – this time frame should range between a few hours at a stretch.

Let's say you put out a bowl in the morning; make sure you've removed it by early afternoon. Likewise, when you put out its evening bowl, make sure you remove it before night falls. The Border Collie will be free to feed as and when it wills during the specified time frame but not otherwise!

Make sure your pet is not going to bed with an empty stomach. If your pet seems to have any particular food preferences, respect these. Food defines your pet's health in the short as well as the long run – make sure it isn't being compromised.

Treats

Since the creation of the first dog treat over 150 years ago the myriad of choices available on every pet store, feed store and grocery store shelf almost outnumbers those looking forward to eating them.

Today's treats are not just for making us guilty humans feel better because it makes us happy to give our fur friends something they really enjoy but today's treats are also designed to actually improve our dog's health.

Some of us humans treat our dogs, others use treats for training purposes, others for health, while still others treat for a combination of reasons.

Whatever reason you choose to give treats to your Border Collie, keep in mind that if we treat our dogs too often throughout the day, we may create a picky eater who will no longer want to eat their regular meals.

As well, if the treats we are giving are high calorie, we may be putting our dog's health in jeopardy by allowing them to become overweight.

Here are a few healthy treats that you can treat your Border Collie with!

Hard Treats

There are so many choices of hard or crunchy treats available that come in many varieties of shapes, sizes and flavors, that you may have a difficult time choosing.

If your Border Collie will eat them, hard treats will help to keep their teeth cleaner. Whatever you do choose, be certain to read the labels and make sure that the ingredients are high quality and appropriately sized for your Border Collie friend.

Soft Treats

Soft, chewy treats are also available in a wide variety of flavors, shapes and sizes for all the different needs of our fur friends and are often used for training purposes as they have a stronger smell.

Dental Treats

Dental treats or chews are designed with the specific purpose of helping your Border Collie to maintain healthy teeth and gums.

They usually require intensive chewing and are often shaped with high ridges and bumps to exercise the jaw and massage gums while removing plaque build-up near the gum line.

Freeze-Dried and Jerky Treats

Freeze-dried and jerky treats offer a tasty morsel most dogs find irresistible as they are usually made of simple, meaty ingredients, such as liver, poultry and seafood. These treats are usually lightweight and easy to carry around, which means they can also be great as training treats.

Human Food Treats

You will want to be very careful when feeding human foods to dogs as treats, because many of our foods contain additives and ingredients that could be toxic and harmful.

Be certain to choose simple, fresh foods with minimal or no processing, such as lean meat, poultry or seafood, and even if your Border Collie will eat anything put in front of them, be aware that many common human foods, such as grapes, raisins, onions and chocolate are poisonous to dogs.

Training Treats

While any sort of treat can be used as an extra incentive during training sessions, soft treats are often used for training purposes because of their stronger smell and smaller sizes.

Yes, we humans love to treat our dogs, whether for helping to teach the new puppy to go pee outside, teaching the adolescent dog new commands, for trick training, for general good behavior, or for no reason at all, other than that they just gave us the "look".

Generally, the treats you feed your dog should not make up more than approximately 10% of their daily food intake, so make sure the treats you choose are high quality, so that you can help to keep your Border Collie both happy and healthy.

Not all treats are healthy for your puppy's consumption. Here are a few harmful treats you should be aware of. Eliminate these from your shopping list to ensure a long and happy life for your Border Collie puppy!

Rawhide

Rawhide is soaked in an ash/lye solution to remove every particle of meat, fat and hair and then further soaked in bleach to remove remaining traces of the ash/lye solution.

Now that the product is no longer food, it no longer has to comply with food regulations. While the hide is still wet it is shaped into rawhide chews, and upon drying it shrinks to approximately 1/4 of its original size.

Further, arsenic based products are often used as preservatives, and antibiotics and insecticides are added to kill bacteria that also fight against good bacteria in your dog's intestines.

The collagen fibers in the rawhide make it very tough and long lasting which makes this chew a popular choice for humans to give to their dogs because it satisfies the dog's natural urge to chew while providing many hours of quiet entertainment.

Sadly, when a dog chews a rawhide treat, they ingest many harsh chemicals and when your dog swallows a piece of rawhide, that piece can swell up to four times its normal size inside your dog's stomach, which can cause anything from mild to severe gastric blockages that could become life threatening and require surgery.

Pigs Ears

These treats are actually the ears of pigs, and while most dogs will eagerly devour them, they are extremely high in fat, which can cause stomach upsets, vomiting and diarrhea for many dogs. Pig ears are often processed and preserved with unhealthy chemicals that discerning dog guardians will not want to feed their dogs. As well, the ears are often quite thin and crispy and when the dog chews them pieces can break off, like chips, and can easily become stuck in a dog's throat. While pig ears are generally not considered to be a healthy treat choice for any dog, they should be especially avoided for any dog that may be at risk of being overweight.

Hoof Treats

Many humans give cow, horse and pig hooves to their dogs as treats because they consider them to be "natural". The truth is that after processing these "treats" they retain little, if any, of their "natural" qualities.

Hoof treats are processed with harsh preservatives, including insecticides, lead, bleach, arsenic based products, and antibiotics to kill bacteria, that can also harm the good bacteria in your dog's intestines, and if these meat-based products are not completely bacteria-free before you feed them to your dog, they could also suffer from Salmonella poisoning.

Hooves can also cause chipping or breaking of your dog's teeth as well as perforation or blockages in your dog's intestines.

Choosing the Right Food

In order to choose the right food for your Border Collie, first, it's important to understand a little bit about canine physiology and what Mother Nature intended when she created our furry friends.

More than 230 years ago, in 1785, the English Sportman's dictionary described the best diet for a dog's health in an article entitled *"Dog"*.

This article indicated that the best food for a dog was something called *"Greaves"*, described as *"the sediment of melted tallow. It is made into cakes for dogs' food. In Scotland and parts of the US it is called cracklings."*

Out of the meager beginning of the first commercially made dog food has sprung a massively lucrative and vastly confusing industry that has only recently begun to evolve beyond those early days of feeding our dogs the dregs of human leftovers because it was cheap and convenient for us humans.

Even today, the majority of dog food choices have far more to do with being convenient for humans to store and serve than it does with being a diet truly designed to be a nutritionally balanced, healthy food choice for a canine.

The dog food industry is very big and as such, because there are now almost limitless choices, there is much confusion and endless debate when it comes to answering the question, *"What is the best food for my dog?"*

Educating yourself, by talking to experts and reading everything you can find on the subject, plus taking into consideration several relevant factors, will help to answer the dog food question for you and your dog.

For instance, where you live may dictate what sorts of foods you have access to. Other factors to consider will include the particular requirements of your dog, such as their age, energy and activity levels.

Next will be the expenses, time and quality. While we all want to give our dogs the best food possible, many humans lead very busy lives and cannot, for instance, prepare their own dog food, but still want to feed their pets a high quality diet that fits within their budget.

However, perhaps most important when choosing an appropriate diet for our dogs, is learning to be more observant of Mother Nature's design and taking a closer look at our dog's teeth, jaws and digestive tract. While humans are omnivores, our canine companions are carnivores, which means that they derive their energy and nutrient requirements from eating a diet consisting of animal proteins.

5. Diet

The Canine Teeth

The first part you should take a good look at when considering what to feed, is your dog's teeth. Unlike humans, who have wide, flat molars for grinding grains, vegetables and other plant-based materials, canine teeth are all pointed because they are designed to rip, shred and tear into animal meat and bone.

The Canine Jaw

Another obvious consideration when choosing an appropriate food source for our furry friends is the fact that every canine is born with powerful jaws and neck muscles to be able to pull down and tear apart their hunted prey. The jaw structure of every canine is such that it opens widely to hold large pieces of meat and bone, while the actual mechanics of a dog's jaw only permits an up-and-down movement that is designed for crushing.

The Digestive Tract

A dog's digestive tract is short and simply designed to move their natural choice of food (hide, meat and bone) quickly through their systems.

Vegetables and plants require more time to break down in the gastrointestinal tract, which in turn, requires a more complex digestive system than what a dog's body is equipped with.

A canine's digestive system is simply unable to break down vegetarian matter, which is why whole vegetables look pretty much the same going into your dog as they do coming out the other end.

Given the choice, most dogs would never choose to eat plants, vegetables or fruits over meat; however, we humans continue to feed them a kibble based diet that contains high amounts of vegetables, fruits and grains and low amounts of meat.

Plus, in order to get our dogs to eat fruits, vegetables and grains we usually have to combine the food with meat or meat by-products.

How healthier would a dog be if we choose to feed them unprocessed and appropriate food?

With hundreds of dog food brands to choose from, it's no wonder we are confused about what to feed our dogs to help them live long and healthy lives.

Following are some suggestions and questions that may help you choose a dog food company that you feel comfortable with:

- How long have they have been in business for?

76

- Is dog food their main product?
- Are they dedicated to their brand?
- Are they easily accessible?
- Do they honestly answer your questions?
- Do they have a good Company Safety Standard?
- Do they set higher standards?
- Read the ingredients - where did they come from?
- Are the ingredients something you would eat?
- Are the ingredients farmed locally?
- Was it cooked using trustworthy standards?
- Is the company certified according to food or organic guidelines?

Whatever you decide to feed your Border Collie, keep in mind that, just as too much wheat, grains and other fillers can have detrimental effects on human health, it can be equally harmful for our furry friends.

Our dogs also suffer from similar life threatening diseases, like heart problems and cancer, rampant in our society, as a direct result of consuming genetically altered, impure, processed and packaged foods.

Raw Diet

While some of us believe we are killing ourselves as well as our dogs with processed foods, others believe that there are dangers associated with raw foods as well.

Raw feeding advocates believe that the ideal diet for their dog is one which would be very similar to what a dog living in the wild would have access to while hunting or foraging. They are often opposed to feeding their dogs any sort of commercially manufactured pet foods, because they consider them to be poor substitutes.

On the other hand, those opposed to feeding their dogs a raw or biologically appropriate raw food diet, believe that the risks associated with food-borne illnesses during the handling and feeding of raw meats outweigh the purported benefits.

Interestingly, even though the United States Food and Drug Administration (FDA) states that they do not advocate a raw diet for dogs, they do advise those who wish to take this route, that following basic hygiene guidelines for handling raw meat can minimize the associated risks.

Further, high pressure pasteurization (HPP), which is high pressure, water based technology for killing bacteria, is USDA-approved for use on organic and natural food products, and is being utilized by many commercial raw pet food manufacturers.

Interestingly, raw meat purchased at your local grocery store contains a much higher level of bacteria than raw food produced at factories. This means that canine guardians feeding their dogs a raw food diet can be quite certain that commercially prepared raw foods sold in pet stores will be safer than raw meats purchased in grocery stores.

Many guardians of high energy, working breed dogs will agree that their dogs thrive on a raw or BARF (Biologically Appropriate Raw Food) diet and strongly believe that there are many potential benefits of such a diet, including:

- healthy, shiny coats
- decreased shedding
- fewer allergy problems
- healthier skin
- cleaner teeth
- fresher breath
- higher energy levels
- improved digestion
- smaller stools
- strengthened immune system
- increased mobility in arthritic pets
- increase or improvement in overall health

Dogs, regardless of their size or breed, are amazing athletes in their own right; therefore every dog deserves to be fed the best available food.

Raw diet is basically what dogs ate before they became domesticated and we turned toward commercially prepared, easy to serve dry dog food that required no special storage or preparation.

The BARF diet is all about feeding our dogs what they are supposed to eat by returning them to their natural, wild diet.

The Dehydrated Diet

Dehydrated dog food comes in both raw and cooked forms and these foods are usually air dried to reduce moisture to a level where bacterial growth is inhibited.

The appearance of de-hydrated dog food is very similar to dry kibble and the typical feeding methods include adding warm water before serving, which makes this type of diet both healthy for our dogs and convenient for us to serve.

Dehydrated recipes are made from minimally processed fresh whole foods to create a healthy and nutritionally balanced meal that meets or exceeds the dietary requirements of a healthy canine. Dehydrating removes only the moisture from the fresh ingredients, which usually means that because the food has not already been cooked at a high temperature, most of the overall nutrition is retained.

A dehydrated diet is a convenient way to feed your dog a nutritious diet because all you have to do is add warm water, and wait five minutes while the food re-hydrates so your Border Collie can enjoy a warm meal.

The Kibble Diet

While many canine owners are taking a closer look at the food choices they are making for their pets, there is no doubt that the convenience and relative economy offered by dry dog food kibble, introduced in the 1940's, continues to make it the most popular pet food choice among dog owners.

Some 75 years later, the massive pet food industry came up with a confusingly large number of choices with hundreds of different manufacturers and brand names lining the shelves of veterinarian offices and pet food aisles at grocery stores.

While feeding a high quality kibble diet that has been flavored to appeal to dogs may keep most Border Collies happy and relatively healthy, you will ultimately need to decide whether this is the best diet for them.

The Right Feeding Bowl

Following is a brief description of the different categories and types of dog bowls that would be appropriate choices for your Border Collie's individual needs.

Automatic Watering Bowls: Standard dog bowls (often made out of plastic) that are attached to a reservoir container, which is designed to keep water constantly available to your dog as long as there is water in the storage compartment.

Ceramic/Stoneware Bowls: An excellent choice for those who like options for design, color and shape.

Elevated Bowls: These raised dining table dog bowls are a tidy and classy choice that will make your dog's dinner time more convenient.

No Skid Bowls: These are for dogs that push their bowls across the floor when eating. A non-skid dog bowl will help keep the feeding bowl where you placed it.

No Tip Bowls: Designed to prevent a messy eater from flipping over their dinner or water bowls.

Stainless Steel Bowls: They are sturdy and sanitary, easy to clean and water stays cool for a longer period of time in a stainless bowl.

Wooden Bowls: For pet owners concerned about stylish home decor, wooden dog bowl dining stations are beautiful pieces of furniture that can enhance your home decor.

Travel Bowls: Convenient, practical and handy additions for every canine travel kit.

Consider a space saving, collapsible dog bowl, made out of hygienic, renewable bamboo that comes in fun colors and different sizes, making it perfect for all travel bowl needs.

If you would like to learn more about the available dog bowl choices, visit DogBowlForYourDog.com, which is a comprehensive, one-stop shop dedicated to explaining the ins and outs of every dog food bowl.

6. Play Time

This is the time your puppy will spend getting entertained by mindless activities. These activities should be carried out by the dog in the play area. This is the place where you will most probably be leaving the puppy without active supervision. It is therefore a natural instinct to puppy-proof this area to the best of your capacity.

Clear the room of all "human" furniture. It'll be a good idea to install a fixed carpet in this room to provide greater stability for its feet. Add in a few toys to this room that your pet likes and is unlikely to choke on and you are done! If there are any windows or doors in the room, make sure you install adequate barriers to keep the puppy in as once it gets bored, it will try to get out and explore "the world beyond"!

Mazes and obstacle courses can stimulate your pet's mind and facilitate its physical as well as mental development. Make sure you invest in your dog's toys wisely – it will define how your pet will look years down the line!

7. Exercise

The Border Collie is an inherently hyper dog and therefore will have a lot of built up energy resource that needs to be expended. A daily walk around a park or in the streets suffices to provide for its exercise needs. However, make sure you are not carrying it in your arms or letting it trot by your side without a leash. The former case kills the purpose of the walk altogether and the latter one accentuates the probability of an escape.

Familiarize your Border Collie with the neighborhood during the first few weeks. This will ensure your Border Collie is able to find its way back if and when it makes a dash into the wilderness. However, never let it off the leash. The cute and amiable appearance of the Border Collie can be dissolved in minutes if the dog feels threatened.

Take it for a walk on a daily basis and make sure you include a weekly or monthly hike in its exercise routine as well. This will not only keep your puppy fit and healthy but also work just the same for you!

8. Travelling

Travel crates are easily the best option available to transport your pet. Make sure it has ample space inside to move a little. Alternatively, the next best option for you is to employ your personal car!

Public transport, though not really prohibited, will not be a very good idea considering its hyperactive nature. If the place is not too far away, walk your canine companion to its destination – it will be able to get its daily dose of exercise. If this isn't possible, avoid putting other people's lives in danger and use your car instead!

Your car might need a few adjustments to accommodate your pet. Nevertheless, it is an investment worth making – especially if you are a frequent traveler!

Remember to add in identification documents to your dog's collar before leaving home and put it on a leash wherever possible. Keep the windows rolled up so your Border Collie does not feel the impulse to escape.

Also, try to keep it on the back seat to prevent it from interfering with your driving. The ideal scenario is to have someone holding the dog and keeping it distracted.

Border Collie dogs get excited by movement. So naturally, having blinds or some toys to keep its eyes away from the windows will be a good idea!

Also, know how your pet signals the call of nature. You definitely do not want reminders of the trip in your car.

Take frequent breaks and walk the Border Collie dog to exhaust its energy reserves. A tired Border Collie is easier to control as compared with one that is full of energy. Improvise along the way as and when required.

There are no hard and fast principles – go with your gut instincts and you should be fine!

After the first few visits, you will automatically find out what more needs to be done to facilitate travels. It isn't a one-time affair. So we suggest you adapt to the rising needs with time!

Chapter 11: House Training Your Border Collie

Most humans believe that they need to take their young dog to puppy classes, and generally speaking, this is a good idea for any young Border Collie (after they have had all their vaccinations), because it will help to get them socialized.

Beyond puppy classes for socializations reasons, hiring a professional dog whisperer for personalized private sessions to train the dog may be far more valuable than training situations where there are multiple dogs and humans together in one class as this can be very distracting for everyone concerned.

The Border Collie is generally well behaved and amiable. But to ensure it follows your orders properly and behaves well in front of other people, you need to put it through a robust training regime. Here are a few things you need to keep in mind while planning for its training regime.

1. Puppy Training Basics

Here are two important and basic aspects of puppy training.

Three Most Important Words

"Come", "Sit" and "Stay" will be the three most important words you will ever teach your Border Collie puppy.

These three basic commands will ensure that your Border Collie remains safe in almost every circumstance.

For instance, when your puppy correctly learns the "Come" command, you can always quickly bring them back to your side if you should see danger be approaching.

When you teach your Border Collie puppy the "Sit" and "Stay" commands you will be further establishing your leadership role. A puppy that understands that their human guardian is their leader will be a safe and happy follower.

Choosing a Discipline Sound

Choosing a "discipline sound" that will be the same for every human family member will make it much easier for your puppy to learn what they can or cannot do and will be very useful when warning your Border Collie puppy before they engage in unwanted behavior.

The best types of sounds are short and sharp so that you and your family members can quickly say them and so that the sound will immediately get the attention of your Border Collie puppy because you want to be able to easily interrupt them when they are about to make a mistake.

It doesn't really matter what the sound is, so long as everyone in the family is consistent.

A sound that is very effective for most puppies and dogs is a simple "UH" sound said sharply and with emphasis.

Most puppies and dogs respond immediately to this sound and if caught in the middle of doing something they are not supposed to be doing will quickly stop and give you their attention or back away from what they were doing.

2. Walking

While walking your Border Collie, never let the dog take lead. If it tries to do so, pull strongly at the leash to warn the pet when it is going out of limits. If it still doesn't obey your wishes, stop for a minute and let it follow suit. It will eventually give in to your wishes.

In the same way, if the Border Collie refuses to move, give it time to rethink its decision. It will eventually pick up and start walking by your side if you persist.

Always keep the Border Collie in a following position. You can allow it to talk by your side but make sure it is not mistaking the signal to mean it is ready to lead. If and when it tries to wander off, all you need to do is manipulate its actions by pulling at the leash.

While walking, it is important for you to keep a steady hold on the leash. At the same time, don't pull too hard or drag the puppy with the leash. You might end up strangling the puppy or causing lasting damage to its tender muscles in the neck region. Don't slack but don't pull too hard either.

Take it for a long walk every day. Choose a specific time of the day when the sun is warm and the environment is breathable. It will be an amazing sight to see your Border Collie trot along your side in utter happiness!

3. Penalizing Unwanted Behaviors

Often humans make the mistake of accidentally rewarding unwanted behaviors.

It is very important to recognize that any attention paid to an overly excited, out of control, adolescent puppy, even negative attention, is likely going to be rewarding for your puppy.

Therefore, when you engage with an out of control Border Collie puppy, you end up actually rewarding them, which will encourage them to continue more of this unwanted behavior.

Be aware that chasing after a puppy when they have taken something they are not supposed to have, picking them up when they are barking or showing aggression, pushing them off when they jump on you or other people, or yelling when they refuse to come when called, are all forms of attention that can actually be rewarding for most puppies.

As your Border Collie dog's guardian, it will be your responsibility to provide calm and consistent structure for your puppy, which will include finding acceptable and safe ways to allow your puppy to vent their energy without being destructive or harmful to property, other dogs, humans, or the actual puppy.

Activities that create or encourage an overly excited Border Collie puppy, such as rough games of tug-o-war, or wild games of chase through the living room, should be immediately curtailed, so that your adolescent puppy learns how to control their energy and play quietly and appropriately without jumping on everyone or engaging in barking or mouthy behavior.

Further, if an adolescent Border Collie puppy displays excited energy simply from being petted by you, your family members or any visitors, you will need to teach yourself, your family and your friends to ignore your puppy until they calm down. Otherwise, you will be teaching your Border Collie puppy that the touch of humans means excitement.

For instance, when you continue to engage with an overly excited puppy, you are rewarding them for uncontrollable behavior and literally teaching them to display energy when they see humans.

Worse, once your puppy has learned that humans are a source of excitement, you will then have to work very hard to reverse this behavior.

Children are often a source of excitement that can cause an adolescent puppy to be extremely wound up.

Do not allow your children to engage with an adolescent Border Collie puppy unless you are there to supervise and teach the children appropriate and calm ways to interact with the puppy.

In order to keep everyone safe, it is very important that your Border Collie puppy learn at an early age that neither children nor adults are sources of excitement.

You can help develop the mind of an adolescent Border Collie and the minds of growing children at the same time by teaching children that your puppy needs structured walks and by showing them how to play fetch, search, hide and seek, or how to teach the Border Collie puppy simple tricks and obedience skills that will be fun and positive interaction for everyone.

4. Maintaining Your Patience

What would you do if your Border Collie dog fails to perform the way you want it to?

Whatever you do, don't shout, holler or physically hurt it. Your Border Collie dog is not a puppet that will follow your orders perfectly every time.

Making mistakes every now and then is perfectly normal for this animal. It will take time and patience to train your Border Collie dog and have it follow your wishes. It does not happen overnight.

So if you are under the impression that training sessions begin yielding results right away, clear the misconception before penalizing your pet.

In any case, if you are penalizing your pet too often on things of no or negligible value, you will end up scarring its personality. The Border Collie dog will become disturbed and develop more behavioral issues. Before getting your pet home, learn to be patient with those that are not subservient to you.

Once you've learnt this valuable trait, only then proceed with your Border Collie purchase. Your pet is not something you can abuse simply because you had a bad time at the office; it is a living being just like you. Care and respect it - that is all that it needs! Training your dog would be easy if we knew the ins and outs of dog training. Here is what you need to do.

5. Perseverance and Consistency

When you enroll your Border Collie in any of the training lessons, make sure you take it in for the session for the entire duration of the course. Just because your pet apparently seems to be behaving well shouldn't encourage you not to take your pet for further sessions.

For the training sessions to be truly effective and long-lasting, it is important for you to remain consistent with the lessons. For all you know, by missing out on any session, you might be reinforcing negative traits in the Border Collie dog.

Take your pet in for the training lessons regularly. It is best if the lessons are done with during its early years. This helps integrate the lessons and values into the pet's behavior, which in turn yields lasting results.

6. Adult Training

The adolescent period in a young Border Collie dog's life, between the ages of 6 and 12 months, is the transitional stage of both physical and psychological development when they are physically almost fully grown in size, yet their minds are still developing and they are testing their boundaries and the limits that their human counterparts will endure.

This can be a dangerous time in a puppy's life because this is when they start to make decisions on their own which, if they do not receive the leadership they need from their human guardians, can lead to developing unwanted behaviors.

When living within a human environment, your puppy must always adhere to human rules and it will be up to their human guardians to continue their vigilant, watchful guidance in order to make sure that they do.

Many humans are lulled into a false sense of security when their new Border Collie puppy reaches the age of approximately six months, because the puppy has been well socialized, they have been to puppy classes and long since been house trained.

The real truth is that the serious work is only now beginning and the humans and their new Border Collie puppy could be in for a time of testing that could seriously challenge the relationship and leave the humans wondering if they made the right decision to share their home with a dog.

If the human side of the relationship is not prepared for this transitional time in their young dog's life, their patience may be seriously tried, and the relationship of trust and respect that has been previously built can be damaged, and could take considerable time to repair.

While not all adolescent puppies will experience a noticeable adolescent period of craziness, because every puppy is different, most young dogs do commonly exhibit at least some of the usual adolescent behaviors, including reverting to previous puppy behaviors.

Some of these adolescent behaviors might include destructive chewing of objects they have previously shown no interest in, selective hearing or ignoring previously learned commands, displaying aggressive behavior, jumping on everyone, barking at everything that moves, or reverting to relieving themselves in the house, even though they were house trained months ago.

Keeping your cool and recognizing these adolescent signs are the first steps toward helping to make this transition period easier on your Border Collie puppy and all family members.

The first step to take that can help keep raging hormones at bay, is to spay or neuter your Border Collie puppy just prior to the onset of adolescence, at around four or five months of age.

While spaying or neutering a Border Collie puppy will not entirely eliminate the adolescent phase, it will certainly help and at the same time will spare your puppy the added strain of both the physical and emotional changes that occur during sexual maturity.

As well, some female puppies will become extremely aggressive toward other dogs during a heat, and non-neutered males may become territorially aggressive and pick fights with other males.

Once your Border Collie puppy has been spayed or neutered, you will want to become more active with your young dog, both mentally and physically by providing them with continued and more complex disciplined exercises.

This can be accomplished by enrolling your adolescent Border Collie in a dog whispering session or more advanced training class, which will help them to continue their socialization skills while also developing their brain.

Even though it may be more difficult to train during this period, having the assistance of a professional and continuing the experience of ongoing socialization amongst other dogs of a similar size can be invaluable, as this is the time when many young dogs begin to show signs of antisocial behavior with other dogs as well as unknown humans.

When your Border Collie is provided with sufficient daily exercise and continued socialization with unfamiliar dogs, people and places that provides interest and expands their mind, they will be able to transition through the adolescent stage of their life much more seamlessly.

7. Human Training

House training, house breaking, or "potty" training, is a critical first step in the education of any new puppy, and the first part of a successful process is training the human guardian.

When you bring home your new Border Collie puppy, they will be relying upon your guidance to teach them what they need to learn.

When you nurture your puppy with consistent patience and understanding, they are capable of learning rules at a very early age, and house training is no different, especially since it's all about establishing a regular routine.

Potty training a new puppy takes time and patience — how much time depends entirely upon you.

Check with yourself and make sure your energy remains consistently calm and patient and that you exercise plenty of compassion and understanding while you help your new puppy learn their new bathroom rules.

Border Collie puppies and dogs flourish with routines and happily, so do humans, therefore, the first step is to establish a daily routine that will work well for both the canine and the human alike.

For instance, depending upon the age of your Border Collie puppy, make a plan to take them out for a toilet break every two hours and stick to it because while you are at the beginning stages of potty training, the more vigilant and consistent you can be, the quicker and more successful your results will be.

Generally speaking, while your puppy is still growing, a young puppy can hold their urge for approximately one hour for every month of their age.

This means if your 2-month-old puppy has been snoozing for a couple of hours, it will need to relieve itself immediately after waking up.

Some of the first indications or signs that your puppy needs to be taken outside to relieve itself will be when you see them:

- sniffing around
- circling
- looking for the door
- whining, crying or barking

- acting agitated

It will be important to always take your Border Collie puppy out first thing every morning, and immediately after they wake up from a nap as well as soon after they have finished eating a meal or having a big drink of water.

Also, your happy praise goes a long way toward encouraging and reinforcing future success when your Border Collie puppy makes the right decisions, so let them know you are happy when they do their business in the right place.

Initially, treats can be a good way to reinforce how pleased you are that your puppy is learning to go potty in the right place. Slowly treats can be removed and replaced with your praise.

Next, now that you have a new puppy in your life, you will want to be flexible with respect to adapting your schedule to meet the requirements that will help to quickly teach your Border Collie puppy their new bathroom routine.

This means not leaving your puppy alone for endless hours at a time because firstly, they are sensitive pack animals that need companionship and your direction at all times, plus long periods alone will result in the disruption of the potty training schedule you have worked hard to establish.

If you have no choice but to leave your puppy alone for many hours, make sure that you place them in a paper lined room or pen where they can relieve themselves without destroying your favorite carpet or new hardwood flooring.

Remember, your Border Collie is a growing puppy with a bladder and bowels that they do not yet have complete control over and you will have a much happier time and better success if you simply train yourself to pay attention to when your young companion is showing signs of needing to relieve themselves.

8. Bell Training

A very easy way to introduce your new Border Collie puppy to house training is to begin by teaching them how to ring a doorbell whenever they need to go outside.

Ringing a doorbell is not only a convenient alert system for both you and your Border Collie puppy or dog, your visitors will be most impressed by how smart your Border Collie is.

A further benefit of training your puppy to ring a bell is that you will not have to listen to your puppy or dog whining, barking or howling to be let out, and your door will not become scratched from their nails.

Unless you prefer to purchase an already manufactured doggy doorbell or system, take a trip to your local novelty store and purchase a small bell that has a nice, loud ring.

Attach the bell to a piece of ribbon or string and hang it from a door handle near the door where you will be taking your puppy out when they need to relieve themselves. The string will need to be long enough so that your Border Collie puppy can easily reach the bell with their nose or a paw.

Next, each time you take your puppy out to go potty, say the word "Out", and use their paw or their nose to ring the bell. Praise them for this "trick" and immediately take them outside.

The only down side to teaching your Border Collie puppy or dog to ring a bell when they want to go outside, is that even if they don't actually have to go out to relieve themselves, but just want to go outside because they are bored, you will still have to take them out every time they ring the bell.

There are many types and styles of "gotta' go" commercially manufactured bells you could choose, ranging from the elegant "Poochie Bells™" that hang from a doorknob, the simple "Tell Bell™" that sits on the floor, or various high tech door chime

94

systems that function much like a doggy intercom system where they push a pad with their paw and it rings a bell.

Whatever doorbell system you choose for your Border Collie puppy, once they are trained, this type of an alert system is an easy way to eliminate accidents in the home.

9. Kennel Training

Kennel training is always a good idea for any puppy early in their education because it can be utilized for many different situations, including keeping them safe while traveling inside a vehicle and being a very helpful tool for house training.

When purchasing a kennel for your Border Collie puppy, always buy a kennel that will be the correct size for your puppy once they become an adult.

The kennel will be the correct size if an adult Border Collie can stand up and easily turn around inside their kennel.

When you train your Border Collie puppy to accept sleeping in their own kennel at nighttime, this will also help to accelerate their potty training, because no puppy or dog wants to relieve themselves where they sleep, which means that they will hold their bladder and bowels as long as they possibly can.

Always be kind and compassionate and remember that a puppy will be able to hold it approximately one hour for every month of their age.

Generally, a Border Collie puppy that is three months old will be able to hold it for approximately three hours, unless they just ate a meal or had a big drink of water.

Be watchful and consistent so that you learn your Border Collie puppy's body language, which will alert you to when it's time for them to go outside.

Presenting them with familiar scents, by taking them to the same spot in the yard or the same street corner, will help to remind and encourage them that they are outside to relieve themselves.

Use a voice cue to remind your puppy why they are outside, such as "go pee" and always remember to praise them every time they relieve themselves in the right place so that they quickly understand what you expect of them and will learn to "go" on cue.

10. Exercise Pen Training

The exercise pen is a transition from kennel only training and will be helpful for those times when you may have to leave your Border Collie puppy for more hours than they can reasonably be expected to hold it.

During those times when you must be away from the home for several hours, it's time to introduce your Border Collie puppy to an exercise pen.

Exercise pens are usually constructed of wire sections that you can put together in whatever shape you desire, and the pen needs to be large enough to hold your puppy's kennel inside one half of the pen, while the other half will be lined with newspapers or pee pads.

Place your Border Collie puppy's food and water dishes next to the kennel and leave the kennel door open, so they can wander in and out whenever they wish, to eat or drink or go to the papers or pads if they need to relieve themselves.

Your puppy will be contained in a small area of your home while you are away and because they are already used to sleeping inside their kennel, they will not want to relieve themselves inside the area where they sleep. Therefore, your Border Collie puppy will naturally go to the other half of the pen to relieve themselves on the newspapers or pee pads.

This method will help train your puppy to be quickly "paper" trained when you must leave them alone for a few hours.

11. Free Training

If you would rather not confine your young Border Collie puppy to one or two rooms in your home, and will be allowing them to freely range about your home anywhere they wish during the day, this is considered free training.

When free house training your Border Collie puppy, you will need to closely watch your puppy's activities all day long so that you can be aware of the "signs" that will indicate when they need to go outside to relieve themselves.

For instance, circling and sniffing is a sure sign that they are looking for a place to do their business.

Never get upset or scold a puppy for having an accident inside the home, because this will result in teaching your puppy to be afraid of you and to only relieve themselves in secret places or when you're not watching.

If you catch your Border Collie puppy making a mistake, all that is necessary is for you to calmly say "No", and quickly scoop them up and take them outside or to their indoor bathroom area.

From your sensitive puppy's point of view, yelling or screaming when they make a potty mistake, will be understood by your puppy or dog as unstable energy being displayed by the person who is supposed to be their leader. This type of unstable behavior will only teach your puppy to fear and disrespect you.

When you are vigilant, the Border Collie is not a difficult puppy to housebreak and they will generally do very well when you start them off with "puppy pee pads" that you will move closer and closer to the same door that you always use when taking them outside. This way they will quickly learn to associate going to this door when they need to relieve themselves.

When you pay close attention to your Border Collie puppy's sleeping, eating, drinking and playing habits, you will quickly learn their body language so that you are able to predict when they might need to relieve themselves.

Your Border Collie puppy will always need to relieve themselves first thing in the morning, as soon as they wake up from a nap, approximately 20 minutes after they finish eating a meal, after they have finished a play session, and of course, before they go to bed at night.

It's important to have compassion during this house training time in your young Border Collie's life so that their education will be as stress-free as possible.

It's also important to be vigilant because how well you pay attention will minimize the opportunities your puppy may have for making a bathroom mistake in the first place, and the fewer mistakes they make, the sooner your Border Collie puppy will be house trained.

12. Electronic Devices Training

Generally speaking, positive training methods are far more effective than using devices that involve negative stimulation.

Further, unless you are training a Border Collie to hunt badgers or rabbits, using electronic devices is usually an excuse for a lazy human who will not take the time to properly train their dog by teaching them rules and boundaries which leads to respect and an attentive follower.

When you do not provide your Border Collie (or any dog) with a consistent leadership role that teaches your dog to trust, respect and listen to you in all circumstances, you will inevitably experience behavioral issues.

Electronic training devices such as e-collars, spray collars or electronic fencing all rely upon negative, painful or stressful reinforcement, which can easily cause a sensitive breed, like the Border Collie, to become nervous or live a life of fear.

For instance, a dog simply cannot understand the principles of "invisible" boundaries, and therefore, should never be subjected to the confusion of the punishment that occurs when walking across an invisible line within their own home territory.

Dogs naturally understand the positive training methods of receiving a reward, which is not only much more efficient and effective when teaching boundaries, rewards are far kinder, and create a much stronger bond with your dog.

The Truth about Shock Collars

First of all, it would have to be an extremely rare situation in which it would be necessary or recommended that you use a shock collar on your Border Collie, as these devices are usually only employed in extreme situations.

The use of remote, electronic, shock or "e-collars" is at best a controversial subject that can quickly escalate into heated arguments.

In certain, rare circumstances, and when used correctly, the e-collar can be a helpful training tool that could actually save a dog's life if they are acting out in dangerous ways.

An e-collar would generally be utilized in a circumstance where a larger breed of dog has access to free range over a large property, resulting in difficulties getting their attention from a distance if they become distracted by other animals or smells.

Many dogs that not been properly trained from a young age also learn that when they are off leash and out of your immediate reach that they can choose to ignore your commands, bark their heads off, terrorize the neighbors or chase wildlife.

Generally e-collars can be effective training tools for working breed herding or hunting or tracking dogs.

In these types of circumstances a remote training collar can be an effective training device for reinforcing verbal commands from a great distance, such as "Come", "Sit" or "Stay".

Finally, electronic collars can be used as a last resort to help teach a dog not to engage in a dangerous behavior that could result in them being seriously harmed or even killed.

Electronic Fencing

Honestly, there are far more reasons NOT to install an electronic fence as a means of keeping your dog inside your yard, than there are good reasons for considering one.

For instance, a dog whose yard is surrounded by an electronic fence can quite easily develop fear, aggression, or both, directed toward what they may believe is the cause of the shock they are receiving.

As a result, installing an electronic fence may cause your Border Collie to become aggressive toward cats, other dogs, other humans, other wildlife, children riding by on bikes or skateboards, the mail carrier, or the dog next door.

As well, a dog that receives a fright, or one who is in a state of excitement forgets about the shock they are going to receive, may run through an electronic fence and then be too frightened or stressed to come back home because it means that they must pass through the painful barrier again.

Further, it is actually possible that electronic fencing may encourage a dog to escape the yard simply because they associate their yard with pain. This feeling can be reinforced if a dog escapes the electronic yard and then is again punished by the shock when they attempt to come home.

The absolute best way to keep your dog safe in their own yard, while helping to establish your role as guardian and leader, is to be out there with them while they are on leash, and to only permit them freedom in your yard under your close supervision.

13. Simple Training Tricks and Tips

When teaching your Border Collie tricks, in order to give them extra incentive, find a treat that they really like, and give the treat as rewards and to help solidify a good performance.

Most dogs will be extra attentive during training sessions when they know that they will be rewarded with their favorite treats.

If your Border Collie is less than six months old when you begin teaching them tricks, keep your training sessions short (no more than 5 or 10 minutes) and fun, and as they become adults, you can extend your sessions as they will be able to maintain their focus for longer periods of time.

Shake a Paw

Who doesn't love a dog that knows how to shake a paw? This is one of the easiest tricks to teach your Border Collie.

TIP: most dogs are naturally either right or left pawed. If you know which paw your dog favors, ask them to shake this paw.

Find a quiet place to practice, without noisy distractions or other pets, and stand or sit in front of your dog. Place them in the sitting position and have a treat in your left hand.

Say the command "Shake" while putting your right hand behind their left or right paw and pulling the paw gently toward yourself until you are holding their paw in your hand. Immediately praise them and give them the treat.

Most dogs will learn the "Shake" trick very quickly, and very soon, once you put out your hand, your Border Collie will immediately lift their paw and put it into your hand, without your assistance or any verbal cue.

Practice every day until they are 100% reliable with this trick, and then it will be time to add another trick to their repertoire.

Roll Over

You will find that just like your Border Collie is naturally either right or left pawed, that they will also naturally want to roll either to the right or the left side. Take advantage of this by asking your dog to roll to the side they naturally prefer.

Sit with your dog on the floor and put them in a lie down position. Hold a treat in your hand and place it close to their nose without allowing them to grab it, and while they are in the lying position, move the treat to the right or left side of their head so that they have to roll over to get to it.

You will very quickly see which side they want to naturally roll to, and once you see this, move the treat to this side. Once they roll over to this side, immediately give them the treat and praise them.

You can say the verbal cue "Over" while you demonstrate the hand signal motion (moving your right hand in a circular motion) or moving the treat from one side of their head to the other with a half circle motion.

Roll Over: moving your right or left arm/hand in a small circular motion, in the direction you wish your dog to roll toward.

Once your Border Collie can roll over every time you ask, it will be time to teach them another trick.

Sit Pretty

While this trick is a little more complicated, and most dogs pick up on it very quickly, remember that every dog is different so always exercise patience.

Find a quiet space with few distractions and sit or stand in front of your dog and ask them to "Sit".

Have a treat nearby (on a countertop or table) and when they sit, use both of your hands to lift up their front paws into the sitting pretty position, while saying the command "Sit Pretty". Help them balance in this position while you praise them and give them the treat.

Once your Border Collie can do the balancing part of the trick quite easily without your help, sit or stand in front of your dog while asking them to "Sit Pretty" and hold the treat above their head, at the level their nose would be when they sit pretty.

TIP: when first beginning this trick, place your Border Collie beside a wall so they can use the wall to help them balance.

If they attempt to stand on their back legs to get the treat, you may be holding the treat too high, which will encourage them to stand on their back legs to reach it. Go back to the first step and put them back into the "Sit" position and again lift their paws while their backside remains on the floor.

Sit Pretty: hold your straight arm, fully extended, over your dog's head with a closed fist.

Make this a fun and entertaining time for your Border Collie and practice a few times every day until they can "Sit Pretty" on hand signal command every time you ask.

A young Border Collie puppy should be able to easily learn these basic tricks before they are six months old and when you are patient and make your training sessions short and fun for your dog, they will be eager to learn more.

14. Handling Mistakes While Training

Remember that a dog's sense of smell is at least 2,000 times more sensitive than a human's. As a result of your Border Collie puppy's superior sense of smell, it will be very important to effectively remove all odors from house training accidents, because otherwise, your Border Collie puppy will be attracted by the smell to the place where they may have had a previous accident, and will want to do their business there again and again.

While there are many products that are supposed to remove odors and stains, many of these are not very effective. You want a professional grade cleaner that will not just mask one odor with another scent; you want a product that will completely neutralize odors.

TIP: go to RemoveUrineOdors.com and order yourself some "SUN" and/or "Max Enzyme" because these products contain professional-strength odor neutralizers and urine digesters that bind to and completely absorb odors on any type of surface.

Chapter 12: Medical Concerns

The medical condition of your dog is another major concern for the health and well being of your pet. Make sure you are reading through this section carefully and are fully aware of your responsibilities as the owner of a Border Collie dog. Any ignorance in this aspect can seriously damage your puppy's health. Here are a couple of things you should keep in mind in this respect.

1. Selecting The Right Veterinarian

A consideration to keep in mind when choosing a veterinarian clinic will be that some clinics specialize in caring for smaller pets, and some specialize in larger animal care, while still others have a wide ranging area of expertise and will care for all animals, including livestock and reptiles.

Choosing a good veterinary clinic will be very similar to choosing the right health care clinic or doctor for your own personal health because you want to ensure that your Border Collie puppy receives the quality care they deserve.

Begin your search by asking other dog owners where they take their furry friends and whether they are happy with the service they receive. If you don't know anyone to ask, visit the local pet store in your area as they should be able to provide you with references and local listings of pet care clinics.

Next, check online, because a good pet clinic will have an active website up and running that will list details of all the services they provide along with an overview of all staff members, their education and qualifications.

Once you've narrowed your search, it's time to personally visit the clinics you may be interested in, as this will be a good opportunity for you to visually inspect the facility, interact with the staff and perhaps meet the veterinarians face to face. Of course, it's not just you who needs to feel comfortable with the clinic chosen and those working there. Your puppy needs to feel comfortable, too, and this is where visiting a clinic and interacting with the staff and veterinarians will provide you with an idea of their experience and expertise in handling your puppy.

If your puppy is comfortable with them, then you will be much more likely to trust that they will be providing the best care for your puppy that will need to receive all their vaccinations and yearly check-ups, and eventually be spayed or neutered.

It's also a good idea to take your puppy into your chosen clinic several times before they actually need to be there for any treatment, so that they are not fearful of the new smells and unfamiliar surroundings.

2. Neutering and Spaying

While it can sometimes be difficult to find the definitive answer when asking when is the best time to neuter or spay your young Border Collie, because there are varying opinions on this topic, one thing that most veterinarians do agree on is that earlier spaying or neutering, between 4 and 6 months of age, is a better choice than waiting. Spaying or neutering surgeries are carried out under general anesthesia, and as more dogs are being neutered at younger ages, speak with your veterinarian and ask for their recommendations regarding the right age to spay or neuter your Border Collie.

Effects on Aggression

Intact (non-neutered) males and females are more likely to display aggression related to sexual behavior than are dogs that have been neutered or spayed.

Fighting, particularly in male dogs that are directed at other males, is less common after neutering, and the intensity of other types of aggression, such as irritable aggression in females will be totally eliminated by spaying.

While neutering or spaying is not a treatment for aggression, it can certainly help to minimize the severity and escalation of aggressiveness and is often the first step toward resolving an aggressive behavior problem.

What is Neutering?

Neutering is a surgical procedure, carried out by a licensed veterinarian surgeon to render a male dog unable to reproduce.

In males, the surgery is also referred to as "castration" because the procedure entails the removal of the young dog's testicles. When the testicles are removed, what is left behind is an empty scrotal sac (which used to contain the puppy's testicles) and this empty sac will soon shrink in size until it is no longer noticeable.

Neutering Males

Neutering male Border Collie puppies before they are six months of age can help to ensure that they will be less likely to suffer from obesity problems when they grow older.

Neutering can also mean that a male Border Collie will be less likely to have the urge to wander.

Further, waiting until a male Border Collie is older than six months before having them neutered could mean that they will experience the effects of raging testosterone that will drive them to escape their yards by any means necessary to search out females to mate with.

Non-neutered males also tend to spray or mark territory much more often, both inside and outside the home, and during this time can start to display aggressive tendencies toward other dogs as well as people.

What is Spaying?

In female puppies, sterilization, referred to as "spaying" is a surgical procedure carried out by a licensed veterinarian, to prevent the female dog from becoming pregnant and to stop regular heat cycles.

The sterilization procedure is much more involved for a female puppy (than for a male), as it requires the removal of both ovaries and the uterus by incision into the puppy's abdominal cavity. The uterus is also removed during this surgery, to prevent the possibility of it becoming infected later on in life.

Spaying Females

Preferably, female Border Collie puppies should be spayed before their very first estrus or heat cycle. Females in heat often appear more agitated and irritable, while sleeping and eating less and some may become extremely aggressive toward other dogs.

Spaying female puppies before their first heat pattern can eliminate these hormonal stressors and reduce the opportunity of mammary glandular tumors. Early spaying also protects against various other potential concerns, such as uterine infections.

Effects on General Temperament

Many dog owners often become needlessly worried that a neutered or spayed dog will lose their vigor.

Rest assured that a dog's personality or energy level will not be modified or altered in any way by the neutering process, and in fact, many unfavorable qualities resulting from hormonal impact may resolve after surgery.

Your Border Collie will certainly not come to be less caring or cheerful, and neither will he or she resent you because you are not denying your dog any essential encounters. You will, however, be acting as a conscientious, informed, and caring Border Collie guardian.

Further, there is little evidence to suggest that the nature of a female Border Collie will improve after having a litter of puppies.

What is important is that you do not project your own psychological needs or concerns onto your Border Collie puppy, because there is no gain to be had from permitting sexual activity in either male or female canines.

For instance, it is not "abnormal" or "mean" to manage a puppy's reproductive activity by having them sterilized. Rather, it is unkind and irresponsible not to neuter or spay a dog and there are many positive benefits of having this procedure carried out.

Effects on Escape and Roaming

A neutered or spayed Border Collie is less likely to wander. Castrated male dogs have the tendency to patrol smaller sized outdoor areas and are less likely to participate in territorial conflicts with perceived opponents.

NOTE: A Border Collie that has actually already experienced successful escapes from the yard may continue to wander after they are spayed or neutered.

Effects on Problem Elimination

An unsterilized dog may urinate or defecate inside the home or in other undesirable areas in an attempt to stake territorial claims, relieve anxiety, or advertise their available reproductive status.

While neutering or spaying a Border Collie puppy after they have already begun to inappropriately eliminate or mark territory to announce their sexual availability to other dogs will reduce the more powerful urine odor as well as eliminate the hormonal factors, once this habit has begun, the undesirable behavior may continue to persist after neutering or spaying.

Possible Weight Gain

While metabolic changes that occur after spaying or neutering can cause some Border Collie puppy's to gain weight, often the real culprit for any weight gain is the human who feels guilty for subjecting their puppy to any kind of pain and therefore, they attempt to make themselves feel better by feeding more treats or meals to their Border Collie companion.

If you are concerned about weight gain after neutering or spaying a Border Collie puppy, simply adjust their food and treat consumption, as needed, and make sure that they receive adequate daily exercise.

It's a very simply process to change your Border Collie dog's food intake according to their physical demands and how they look, and if your Border Collie puppy's daily exercise and level of activity has not changed after they have been spayed or neutered, there will likely be no change in food management necessary.

3. Importance of Vaccinations

Puppies need to be vaccinated by a veterinarian in order to provide them with protection against four common and serious diseases. Vaccination against this common set of diseases is referred to as "DAPP", which stands for Distemper, Adenovirus, Parainfluenza and Parvo Virus.

Approximately one week after your Border Collie puppy has completed all three sets of primary DAPP vaccinations they will be fully protected from those specific diseases. Thereafter, most veterinarians will recommend a once a year vaccination for the next year or two. It has now become common practice to vaccinate adult dogs every three years, and if your veterinarian is insisting on a yearly vaccination for your Border Collie puppy, you need to ask them why, because to do otherwise is considered by most professionals to be "over vaccinating".

Distemper

Canine distemper is a contagious and serious viral illness for which there is currently no known cure.

This deadly virus, which is spread either through the air or by direct or indirect contact with a dog that is already infected or other distemper carrying wildlife, including ferrets, raccoons, foxes, skunks and wolves, is a relative of the measles virus which affects humans.

Canine distemper is sometimes also called "hard pad disease" because some strains of the distemper virus actually cause thickening of the pads on a dog's feet, which can also affect the end of a dog's nose.

In dogs or animals with weak immune systems, death may result two to five weeks after the initial distemper infection.

Early symptoms of distemper include fever, loss of appetite, and mild eye inflammation that may only last a day or two. Symptoms become more serious and noticeable as the disease progresses.

A puppy or dog that survives the distemper virus will usually continue to experience symptoms or signs of the disease throughout their remaining lifespan, including "hard pad disease" as well as "enamel hypoplasia", which is damage to the enamel of the puppy's teeth that are not yet formed or that have not yet pushed through the gums.

Enamel hypoplasia is caused when the distemper virus kills the cells that manufacture tooth enamel.

Adenovirus

It is a virus that causes infectious canine hepatitis, which can range in severity from very mild to very serious, sometimes resulting in death.

Symptoms can include coughing, loss of appetite, increased thirst and urination, tiredness, runny eyes and nose, vomiting, bruising or bleeding under the skin, swelling of the head, neck and body, fluid accumulation in the abdomen area, jaundice (yellow tinge to the skin), a bluish clouding of the cornea of the eye (called "hepatitis blue eye") and seizures.

There is no specific treatment for infectious canine hepatitis. Treatment of the disease is focused on managing symptoms while the virus runs its course. Hospitalization and intravenous fluid therapy may be required in severe cases.

Canine Parainfluenza Virus

The canine parainfluenza virus (CPIV) also referred to as "canine influenza virus", "greyhound disease" or "race flu", which is easily spread through the air or by coming into contact with respiratory secretions, was originally a virus that only affected horses.

This disease is believed to have adapted to become contagious to dogs, is easily spread from dog to dog, and may cause symptoms that become fatal.

While the more frequent occurrences of this respiratory infection are seen in areas where there are high dog populations, such as race tracks, boarding kennels and pet stores, this virus is highly contagious to any dog or puppy, at any age.

Symptoms can include a dry, hacking cough, difficulty breathing, wheezing, runny nose and eyes, sneezing, fever, loss of appetite, tiredness, depression and possible pneumonia.

In cases where only a cough exists, tests will be required to determine whether the cause of the cough is the parainfluenza virus or the less serious "kennel cough".

While many dogs can naturally recover from this virus, they will remain contagious, and for this reason, in order to prevent the spread to other animals, aggressive treatment of the virus, with antibiotics and antiviral drugs will be the general course of action.

In more severe cases, a cough suppressant may be prescribed, as well as intravenous fluids to help prevent secondary bacterial infection.

Canine Parvovirus

Canine parvovirus (CPV) is a highly contagious viral illness affecting puppies and dogs. Parvovirus also affects other canine species including foxes, coyotes and wolves.

There are two forms of this virus (1) the more common intestinal form, and (2) the less common cardiac form, which can cause death in young puppies.

Symptoms of the intestinal form of parvovirus include vomiting, bloody diarrhea, weight loss, and lack of appetite, while the less common cardiac form attacks the heart muscle.

Early vaccination in young puppies has radically reduced the incidence of canine parvovirus infection, which is easily transmitted either by direct contact with an infected dog, or indirectly, by sniffing an infected dog's feces.

The virus can also be brought into a dog's environment on the bottom of human shoes that may have stepped on infected feces, and there is evidence that this hardy virus can live in ground soil for up to a year.

Recovery from parvovirus requires both aggressive and early treatment. With proper treatment, death rates are relatively low (between 5 and 20%), although chances of survival for puppies are much lower than for older dogs, and in all instances, there is no guarantee of survival.

Treatment of parvovirus requires hospitalization where intravenous fluids and nutrients are administered to help combat dehydration. As well, antibiotics will be given to counteract secondary bacterial infections, and as necessary, medications to control nausea and vomiting may also be given.

Without prompt and proper treatment, dogs that have severe parvovirus infections can die within 48 to 72 hours.

4. Diseases and viruses your Border Collie is prone to

Rabies

Rabies is a viral disease transmitted by coming into contact with the saliva of an infected animal, usually through a bite. The virus travels to the brain along the nerves and once symptoms develop, death is almost certainly inevitable, usually following a prolonged period of suffering.

If you plan to travel out of State or across country borders, you will need to make sure that your Border Collie has an up to date Rabies Vaccination Certificate (NASPHV form 51) indicating they have been inoculated against rabies.

Vaccinating dogs against rabies is also compulsory in most countries in mainland Europe, as is permanent identification and registration of dogs through the use of a Pet Passport. Those living in a country that is rabies free (UK, Eire) are not required to vaccinate their dogs against rabies, unless they intend to travel.

Leishmaniasis

Leishmaniasis is caused by a parasite and is transmitted by a bite from a sand fly. There is no definitive answer for effectively combating Leishmaniasis, especially since one vaccine will not prevent the known multiple species.

In areas where the known cause is a sand fly, deltamethrin collars (containing a neurotoxic insecticide) worn by the dogs has been proven to be 86% effective.

There are two types of Leishmaniasis: (1) a skin reaction causing hair loss, lesions and ulcerative dermatitis, and (2) a more severe, abdominal organ reaction, which is also known as "black fever".

When the disease affects organs of the abdominal cavity the symptoms include:

- Loss of appetite
- Diarrhea
- Severe weight loss
- Exercise intolerance
- Vomiting
- Nose bleed
- Tarry feces
- Fever
- Pain in the joints
- Excessive thirst and urination
- Inflammation of the muscles

Leishmaniasis spreads throughout the body to most organs, with kidney failure being the most common cause of death. Virtually all infected dogs develop this system wide disease and as much as 90% of those infected will also display skin reactions.

Affected dogs in the US are frequently found to have acquired this infection in another country.

Of note, is that this disease is regularly found in the Middle East, the area around the Mediterranean basin, Portugal, Spain, Africa, South and Central America, southern Mexico and the US, with regular cases reported in Oklahoma and Ohio, where it is found in 20 to 40% of the dog population.

There have also been a few reported cases in Switzerland, northern France and the Netherlands.

NOTE: Leishmaniasis is a "zoonotic" infection, which is a contagious disease that can be spread between both animals and humans. This means that the organisms residing in the Leishmaniasis lesions can be communicated to humans.

Treatment in dogs is often difficult and the dog may suffer from relapses. Leishmaniasis poses a significant risk to the health of your dog, especially if you travel to the Mediterranean.

Lyme disease

This is one of the most common tick-borne diseases in the world, which is transmitted by Borrelia bacteria found in the deer or sheep tick.

Lyme disease, also called "borreliosis", is also a zoonotic disease that can affect both humans and dogs and this disease can be fatal.

The Borrelia bacteria that causes Lyme's disease, is transmitted by slow-feeding, hard-shelled deer or sheep ticks, and the tick usually has to be attached to the dog for a minimum of 18 hours before the infection is transmitted.

Symptoms of this disease in a young or adult dog include:

- Recurrent lameness from joint inflammation
- Lack of appetite
- Depression
- Stiff walk with arched back
- Sensitivity to touch
- Swollen lymph nodes
- Fever
- Kidney damage
- Rare heart or nervous system complications

While Lyme disease has been reported in dogs throughout the United States and Europe, it is most prevalent in the upper Mid-Western states, the Atlantic seaboard, and the Pacific coastal states.

In order to properly diagnose and treat Lyme disease, blood tests will be required, and if the tests are positive, oral antibiotics will be prescribed to treat the conditions.

Prevention is the key to keeping this disease under control because dogs that have had Lyme disease before are still able to get the disease again.

There is a vaccine for Lyme disease and dogs living in areas that have easy access to these ticks should be vaccinated yearly.

Rocky Mountain spotted fever

This tick-transmitted disease is very often seen in dogs in the East, Midwest, and plains region of the US, and the organisms causing Rocky Mountain Spotted Fever (RMSF) are transmitted by both the American dog tick and the RMSF tick, which must be attached to the dog for a minimum of five hours in order to transmit the disease.

Common symptoms of RMSF include:

- Fever
- Reduced appetite
- Depression
- Pain in the joints
- Lameness
- Vomiting
- Diarrhea

Some dogs affected with RMSF may develop heart abnormalities, pneumonia, kidney failure, liver damage, or even neurological signs, such as seizures or unsteady, wobbly or stumbling gait. Diagnosis of this disease requires blood testing and if the results are positive, oral antibiotics will be given to the infected dog for approximately two weeks. Dogs that can clear the organism from their systems will recover and after being infected, will remain immune to future infection.

Ehrlichiosis

This is another tick borne disease transmitted by both the brown dog tick and the Lone Star Tick. Ehrlichiosis has been reported in every state in the US, as well as worldwide. Common symptoms include:

- Depression
- Reduced appetite
- Fever
- Stiff and painful joints
- Bruising

Signs of infection typically occur less than a month after a tick bite and last for approximately four weeks. There is no vaccine available. Blood tests may be required to test for antibodies and treatment will require a course of antibiotics for up to four weeks in order to completely clear the organism from the infected dog's system.

After a dog has been previously infected, they may develop antibodies to the organism, but will not be immune to being re-infected.

Dogs living in areas of the country where the Ehrlichiosis tick diseases are common or widespread may be prescribed low doses of antibiotics during tick season.

Anaplasmosis

Deer ticks and western blacklegged ticks are carriers of the bacteria that transmit canine Anaplasmosis.

However, there is also another form of Anaplasmosis (caused by different bacteria) that is carried by the brown dog tick. Because the deer tick also carries other diseases, some animals may be at risk for developing more than one tick-borne disease at the same time.

Signs of Anaplasmosis are similar to Ehrlichiosis and include painful joints, diarrhea, fever, and vomiting as well as possible nervous system disorders.

A dog will usually begin to show signs of Anaplasmosis within a couple of weeks after infection and diagnosis will require blood and urine testing, and sometimes other specialized laboratory tests.

Treatment is with oral antibiotics for up to 30 days, depending on how severe the infection may be.

When this disease is quickly treated, most dogs will recover completely, however, subsequent immunity is not guaranteed, which means that a dog may be re-infected if exposed again.

Tick Paralysis

Tick paralysis is caused when ticks secrete a toxin that affects the nervous system.

Affected dogs show signs of weakness and limpness approximately one week after being first bitten by ticks.

Symptoms usual begin with a change in pitch of the dog's usual bark, which will become softer, and weakness in the rear legs that eventually involves all four legs, which is then followed by the dog showing difficulty breathing and swallowing.

If the condition is not diagnosed and properly treated, death can occur.

Treatment involves locating and removing the tick and then treating the infected dog with tick anti-serum.

Canine Coronavirus

While this highly contagious intestinal disease, which is spread through the feces of contaminated dogs, was first discovered in Germany during 1971 when there was an outbreak in sentry dogs, it is now found worldwide.

This virus can be destroyed by most commonly available disinfectants.

Symptoms include:

- Diarrhea
- Vomiting
- Weight loss or anorexia

While deaths resulting from this disease are rare, and treatment generally requires only medication to relieve the diarrhea, dogs that are more severely affected may require intravenous fluids to combat dehydration.

There is a vaccine available, which is usually given to puppies, because they are more susceptible at a young age. This vaccine is also given to show dogs that have a higher risk of exposure to the disease.

Leptospirosis

This is a disease that occurs throughout the world that can affect many different kinds of animals, including dogs, and as it is also a zoonotic disease, this means that it can affect humans, too. There is potential for both dogs and humans to die from this disease.

The disease is always present in the environment, which makes it easy for any dog to pick up. This is because it is found in many common animals, such as rats, and wildlife, as well as domestic livestock.

Veterinarians generally see more cases of Leptospirosis in the late summer and fall, which is probably because that is when more pets and wildlife are out and about.

More cases also occur after heavy rain falls.

The disease is most common in mild or tropical climates around the World, and in the US or Canada, it is more common in states or provinces that receive heavy rainfall.

The good news is that you can protect your dog from leptospirosis by vaccination, and while puppies are not routinely vaccinated against leptospirosis because chances of contracting the disease depends upon the lifestyle of the dog as well as the area in which the dog lives, it makes sense to vaccinate against this disease if you and your dog do live in an area considered a hot spot for leptospirosis, so ask your veterinarian.

City rat populations are a major carrier of leptospirosis. Cold winter conditions lower the risk because the leptospira organisms do not tolerate the freezing and thawing of near-zero temperatures.

They are killed rapidly by drying, but they persist in standing water, dampness, mud and alkaline conditions. Most of the infected wild animals and domestic animals that spread leptospirosis do not appear ill.

The leptospira take up residence in the kidneys of infected animals, which can include rats, mice, squirrels, skunks, and raccoons and when these animals void urine, they contaminate their environment with living leptospira.

Dogs usually become infected after sniffing urine or by wading, swimming or drinking contaminated water that has infected urine in it, and this is how the disease passes from animal to animal.

As well, the leptospira can also enter through a bite wound or if a dog eats infected material.

5. Additional Vaccinations

Depending upon where you and your Border Collie live, your veterinarian may suggest additional vaccinations to help combat diseases that may be more common in your area.

The first vaccination needle is normally given to a puppy around six to eight weeks of age, which means that generally it will be the responsibility of the Border Collie breeder to ensure that the puppy's first shots have been received before their new owner takes them home.

Thereafter, it will be the new Border Collie puppy's guardians that will be responsible for ensuring that the next two sets of shots, which are usually given three to four weeks after each other, are given by the new guardian's veterinarian at the proper intervals.

6. De-Worming the Dog

De-worming kills internal parasites that your dog or puppy may have.

NOTE: no matter how sanitary your conditions are, or where you live, your dog will have internal parasites, because it is not a matter of cleanliness.

It is recommended by the Center for Disease Control (CDC) that puppies should be de-wormed every 2 weeks until they are 3 months old, and then every month after that, in order to control worms. Many veterinarians recommend checking dogs for tapeworms and roundworms every 6-12 months.

7. Poison Control

Knowing Poisonous Foods

While some dogs are smart enough to avoid foods that can harm or kill them, other canines eagerly eat absolutely anything they get.

As conscientious guardians for our furry friends, it will always be our responsibility to make certain that when we share our homes with a dog, we never leave food items that could be toxic or lethal to them within their reach.

While there are many foods that can be toxic to a Border Collie, the following alphabetical list contains some of the more common foods that can seriously harm or even kill your dogs including:

Bread Dough: If your dog eats bread dough, their body heat will cause the dough to rise inside the stomach. As the dough expands during the rising process, alcohol is produced.

Dogs who have eaten bread dough may experience stomach bloating, abdominal pain, vomiting, disorientation and depression. Because bread dough can rise to many times its original size, eating only a small amount will cause a problem for any dog.

Broccoli: Isothiocynate is the toxic ingredient in broccoli. While it may cause an upset stomach, it probably won't be very harmful unless the amount eaten is more than 10% of the dog's total daily diet.

Chocolate: Contains theobromine, a chemical that is toxic to dogs when consumed in large quantities. Chocolate also contains caffeine, which is also found in coffee, tea, and certain soft drinks. Different types of chocolate contain different amounts of theobromine and caffeine.

For example, dark chocolate and baking chocolate or cocoa powder contain more of these compounds than milk chocolate does, therefore, it would take more milk chocolate to adversely affect a dog.

However, even a few ounces of chocolate can be enough to cause illnesses or death in puppies or smaller dogs, like the Border Collies, therefore, no amount or type of chocolate should be considered safe for a dog to eat.

Chocolate toxicity can cause vomiting, diarrhea, rapid or irregular heart rate, restlessness, muscle tremors, and seizures. Death can occur within 24 hours of eating in more serious cases.

Chocolate is often more easily available to curious dogs during festive seasons such as Christmas, New Year, Valentine's, Easter and Halloween, especially through children who are not so careful with where they keep their Halloween or Easter candy stash, making it an easy mark for a hungry dog.

In some cases, people unconsciously poison their dogs by offering them chocolate as a treat or leaving chocolate cookies or frosted cake within licking distance.

Caffeine: Beverages containing caffeine, such as soda, tea, coffee, and chocolate, act as a stimulant and can accelerate your dog's heartbeat to a dangerous level. Dogs who have consumed caffeine have been reported to have seizures, some of which have proven to be fatal.

Cooked Bones: Can be extremely hazardous for a dog because bones become brittle when cooked which causes them to splinter when the dog chews on them.

Splinters have sharp edges that can get stuck in their teeth, cause choking, or create a rupture or puncture of the stomach lining or intestinal tract.

Especially dangerous are cooked turkey and chicken legs, ham, pork chop and veal bones. Symptoms of choking include:

- Pale or blue gums
- Gasping open-mouthed breathing
- Pawing at the face
- Slow, shallow breathing
- Falling unconscious with dilated pupils

Grapes and Raisins: Can cause acute kidney failure in dogs. While it is not known what the toxic agent is in this fruit, clinical signs can occur within 24 hours of eating and include vomiting, diarrhea, and lethargy.

Other signs of illness caused from eating grapes or raisins relate to an eventual shutdown of kidney functions.

Garlic and Onions: Contain chemicals that damage red blood cells by rupturing them so they lose their ability to carry oxygen effectively, which leaves the dog short of oxygen, causing what is called "hemolytic anemia".

Poisoning can occur with a single ingestion of large quantities of garlic or onions or with repeated meals containing small amounts. Cooking does not reduce the potential toxicity of onions and garlic.

NOTE: Fresh, cooked, and/or powdered garlic or onions are commonly found in baby food, which is sometimes given to dogs when they are sick, therefore, be certain to carefully read food labels before feeding them to your Border Collie.

Macadamia Nuts: are commonly found in candy and chocolates. Although the reasons behind macadamia nut toxicity are not well understood, reactions include depression, weakness, vomiting, tremors, joint pain, and pale gums.

Signs can occur within 12 hours of eating. In some cases, symptoms can resolve themselves without treatment within 24 to 48 hours, however, keeping a close eye on your Border Collie is strongly recommended.

Mushrooms: Mushroom poisoning can be fatal if certain species of mushrooms are eaten.

The most commonly reported toxic species of mushroom in the US is Amanita phalloides (Death Cap mushroom), which is also quite a common species found in most parts of Britain. Other Amanita species are also toxic.

This deadly mushroom is often found growing in grassy or wooden areas near various deciduous and coniferous trees, which mean that if you're out walking with your Border Collie in the woods, they could easily find these mushrooms.

Eating them can cause severe liver disease and neurological disorders. If you suspect your dog has eaten these mushrooms, immediately take them to a veterinarian, as the recommended treatment is to induce vomiting and to give activated charcoal. Further treatment for liver disease may also be necessary.

Pits and Seeds: Many seeds and pits found in a variety of fruits, including apples, apricots, cherries, pears and plums, contain cyanogenic glycosides that can cause cyanide poisoning in your Border Collie.

The symptoms of cyanide poisoning usually occur within 15-20 minutes to a few hours after eating and symptoms can include initial excitement, followed by rapid respiration rate, salivation, voiding of urine and feces, vomiting, muscle spasm, staggering, and coma before death.

Dogs suffering from cyanide poisoning that live more than 2 hours after onset of symptoms will usually recover.

Raw Salmon or Trout: Salmon Poisoning Disease (SPD) can be a problem for anyone who goes fishing with their dog, or feeds their dog a raw meat diet that includes raw salmon or trout.

When a snail is infected and then is eaten by the fish, as part of the food chain, the dog is exposed when it eats the infected fish.

A sudden onset of symptoms can occur 5-7 days after eating the infected fish. In the acute stages, gastrointestinal symptoms are quite similar to canine parvovirus.

SPD has a mortality rate of up to 90%, can be diagnosed with a fecal sample and is treatable if caught in time.

Prevention is simple, cook the fish before feeding it to your Border Collie and immediately see your veterinarian if you suspect that your dog has eaten raw salmon or trout.

Tobacco: All forms of tobacco, including patches, nicotine gum and chewing tobacco can be fatal to dogs if eaten.

Signs of poisoning can appear within an hour and include hyperactivity, salivation, panting, vomiting and diarrhea.

Advanced signs include muscle weakness, twitching, collapse, coma, increased heart rate and eventually cardiac arrest.

Never leave tobacco products within reach of your Border Collie, and be careful not to let them pick up discarded cigarette butts when they are young puppies.

If you suspect your dog has eaten any of these, seek immediate medical help.

TIP: When your Border Collie is very young, use a double leash, collar and harness arrangement, so that you can still teach them to walk on a leash with a Martingale collar around their neck, but can also attach the second leash to their harness so that you can easily lift them over enticing cigarette butts or other toxic garbage they may be trying to eat during walks.

Tomatoes: Contain atropine, which can cause dilated pupils, tremors and irregular heartbeat. The highest concentration of atropine is found in the leaves and stems of tomato plants, next is the unripe (green) tomatoes, followed by the ripe tomato.

Xylitol: is an artificial sweetener found in products such as gum, candy, mints, toothpaste, and mouthwash that is recognized by the National Animal Poison Control Center to be a risk to dogs.

Xylitol is harmful to dogs because it causes a sudden release of insulin in the body that leads to hypoglycemia (low blood sugar). Xylitol can also cause liver damage in dogs.

Within 30 minutes after eating a product containing xylitol, the dog may vomit, be lethargic (tired), and/or be uncoordinated. However, some signs of toxicity can also be delayed for hours or even for a few days. Xylitol toxicity in dogs can be fatal if left untreated.

Please be aware that the above list is just some of the more common foods that can be toxic or fatal to our fur friends and that there are many other foods we should never be feeding our dogs.

If you have one of those dogs who will happily eat anything that looks or smells like food, be certain to keep these foods far away from your beloved Border Collie and you'll help them to live a long and healthy life.

Poisonous Plants inside Your Home

Many common house plants are actually poisonous to our canine companions, and although many dogs simply ignore house plants, some will attempt to eat anything, especially puppies who want to taste everything in their new world.

More than 700 plant species contain toxins that may harm or be fatal to puppies or dogs, depending on the size of the puppy or dog and how much they may eat. It will be especially important to be aware of household plants that could be toxic when you are sharing your home with a new puppy.

Following is a short list of the more common household plants, what they look like, the different names they are known by, and what symptoms would be apparent if your puppy or dog ingests them.

Aloe Plant: Medicine plant or Barbados aloe, is a very common succulent that is toxic to dogs. The toxic agent in this plant is Aloin. This bitter yellow substance is found in most aloe species and may cause vomiting and/or reddish urine.

Asparagus Fern (Emerald feather, Emerald fern, Sprengeri fern, Plumosa fern, Lace fern): The toxic agent in this plant is sapogenin — a steroid found in a variety of plants. Berries from this plant can cause vomiting, diarrhea and abdominal pain among dogs. Skin inflammation from repeated exposure is another side effect of this plant.

Corn Plant: Its sub-types, cornstalk plant, dracaena, dragon tree, and ribbon plant are all toxic to dogs. Saponin is the harmful chemical compound found in this plant. If the plant is eaten, vomiting (with or without blood), loss of appetite, depression and/or increased salivation can occur.

Cyclamen: Sowbread is a pretty, flowering plant that, if eaten, can cause increased salivation, vomiting and diarrhea. If a dog eats a large amount of the plant's tubers, which are usually found below the soil at the root — heart rhythm abnormalities, seizures and even death can occur.

Dieffenbachia (dumb cane, tropic snow, exotica): Contains a chemical that is a poisonous deterrent to animals. If the plant is eaten, oral irritation can occur, especially on the tongue and lips. This irritation can lead to increased salivation, difficulty swallowing and vomiting.

Elephant Ear (caladium, taro, pai, ape, cape, via, via sori, malanga): Contains a chemical similar to that found in dieffenbachia, therefore, a dog's reaction to elephant ear is similar: oral irritation, increased salivation, difficulty swallowing and vomiting.

Heartleaf Philodendron: Its sub-types, horsehead philodendron, cordatum, fiddle leaf, panda plant, split-leaf philodendron, fruit salad plant, red emerald, red princess, and saddle leaf, are all common, easy-to-grow houseplants that contain a chemical that irritates the mouth, tongue and lips of dogs. An affected dog may also experience increased salivation, vomiting and difficulty in swallowing.

Jade Plant (baby jade, dwarf rubber plant, jade tree, Chinese rubber plant, Japanese rubber plant, friendship tree): While the toxic property in this plant is unknown, eating it can cause depression, loss of coordination and, although rare, a slow heart rate.

Lilies: some plants of the lily family are toxic to dogs. The peace lily (also known as Mauna Loa) is toxic to dogs. Eating the peace lily or calla lily can cause irritation of the tongue and lips, increased salivation, difficulty in swallowing and vomiting.

Satin Pothos: Also known as silk pothos, if eaten by a dog, the plant may cause irritation to the mouth, lips and tongue, while the dog may also experience increased salivation, vomiting and/or difficulty in swallowing.

The plants noted above are only a few of the more common household plants, and every conscientious Border Collie guardian will want to educate themselves before bringing plants into the home that could be toxic to their canine companions.

Poisonous Garden Plants

Please note that there are also many outdoor plants that can be toxic or poisonous to your Border Collie therefore, always check what plants are growing in your garden and if there are any that may be harmful, remove them or ascertain that your Border Collie puppy or adult dog does not eat them. Cornell University's Department of Animal Science lists many different categories of poisonous plants affecting dogs, including house plants, flower garden plants, vegetable garden plants, plants found in swamps or moist areas, plants found in fields, trees and shrubs, plants found in wooded areas, and ornamental plants.

Poison Proofing

You can learn about many potentially toxic and poisonous sources both inside and outside your home by visiting the ASPCA Animal Poison Control Center website.

Always keep your veterinarian's emergency number in a place where you can quickly access it, as well as the Emergency Poison Control telephone number; in case you suspect that your dog may have been poisoned.

Knowing what to do if you suspect your dog may have been poisoned and being able to quickly contact the right people could save your Border Collie's life.

If you keep toxic cleaning substances (including fertilizers, vermin or snail poisons and vehicle products) in your home or garage, always keep them behind closed doors.

Also, keep any medications away, and seriously consider eliminating the use of any and all toxic products, for both you and your dog's health.

Symptoms of Poisoning

It is impossible to keep a check over your pet at all times. Naturally, it opens a window of opportunity for your pet to explore around your place. And when it is on this mission, it seldom will respect the boundaries you set for your pet.

On its exploration spree, it can come into contact with or try to ingest those items that can cause poisoning.

Here are some of the symptoms you should look out for that point towards the possibility of poisoning. So even if you were not on guard, you can save your pet by rushing it to the vet in time.

Abdominal pain
Your dog will suddenly begin to whine a lot and when you try to touch its abdomen, you will feel it has become tender.

Coma
Your canine friend will refuse to respond to your orders and will remain in a subconscious state for extended periods of time. When this happens, you should absolutely take no time to get it to

a veterinary doctor as this symbolizes an aggravated stage of poisoning.

Convulsions
Poison can trigger convulsions in your pet. Rush it to the vet immediately if your pet begins to convulse all of a sudden.

Diarrhea
Poison can disrupt its digestive system. So if you see unexplained loose stools, rush to a poison control center or a vet immediately. Admittedly, this is a much "lighter" version of poisoning. Nevertheless, untimely help can lead it to a horrific fate.

Drooling
It is not much of a problem as most Border Collie dogs are likely to drool. It is normal for quite a few. However, if you observe your Border Collie dog has suddenly started drooling even though it did not do so before, consult a vet.

Irregular heartbeat
Placing a hand on its chest will tell you if its heartbeats are normal or not.
Like humans, the heartbeats are quite superficial. If you see your Border Collie dog exhibiting some of the aforementioned characteristics, immediately roll it over and feel for its heartbeat. If it is irregular, you know what you need to do!

Difficulty breathing
It will become evident to you when and if your pet is facing difficulty breathing. It will be making a conscious effort to keep breathing and will refuse to perform any strenuous activities. This will become even more evident if you observe it closely for a few minutes while it is lying on the floor.

Fatigue
If your canine companion feels tired, it will automatically show on its face.
Just keep a close eye on his reactions. Any deviation from normalcy is almost always an indicator of trouble.

Swollen limbs

Toxins in poisons can cause swelling in its limbs as well as in its internal organs. If it becomes apparent on its limbs, rush it to the emergency services immediately. You never know if internal swelling like that on its windpipe might become a major threat to its survival.

Vomiting

Anything that is not tolerated well by its body is likely to be expelled in the form of vomit. However, this does not happen every time it tries to ingest poison. If you are sure there is absolutely no other reason why your pet should begin vomiting all of a sudden, rush it to the vet immediately. A stitch in time saves nine!

If you observe any or all of these symptoms in your pet and you know that they are not normal for it, consult a veterinarian immediately. If it is too difficult to seek out a veterinarian, look for the nearest poison control center for dogs. In such a situation, time is extremely sensitive to your pet's health. So don't procrastinate and don't take any chances.

Your pet deserves the best so make sure you don't let it down on this!

Animal Poison Control Centers

The ASPCA Animal Poison Control Center is staffed 24 hours a day, 365 days a year and is a valuable resource for learning about what plants are toxic and possibly poisonous to your dog.

a) USA Poison Emergency
Call: 1 (888) 426-4435
When calling the Poison Emergency number, a $65 (£39.42) consultation fee may be applied to your credit card.

b) UK Poison Emergency

Call: 0800-213-6680 - Pet Poison Helpline (payable service)

Call: 0300 1234 999 - RSPCA

www.aspca.org = ASPCA Poison Control.

8. Licensing

Many cities and jurisdictions around the world require that dogs be licensed.

Usually a dog license is an identifying tag that the dog will be required to wear on their collar. The tag will have an identifying number and a contact number for the registering organization, so that if someone finds a lost dog wearing a tag, the owner of the dog can be contacted.

Most dog tags are only valid for one year, and will need to be renewed annually at the beginning of every New Year, which involves paying a fee, which can vary from jurisdiction to jurisdiction. From one extreme to the next, owners of dogs living in Beijing, China must pay a licensing fee of $600 (£411), while those living in Great Britain require no fee, because licensing of dogs was abolished in 1987.

Ireland and Northern Ireland both require dogs to be licensed and in Germany dog ownership is taxed, rather than requiring licensing, with higher taxes being paid for breeds of dogs deemed to be "dangerous".

Most US states and municipalities have licensing laws in effect and Canadian, Australian and New Zealand dogs also must be licensed, with the yearly fee approximately $30 to $50 (£20 to £35) depending upon whether the dog has been spayed or neutered.

Tattooing

Dogs are tattooed to help identify them in case they are lost or stolen and many dog guardians prefer this safe, simple solution over micro-chipping.

Tattooing does not require locating a scanner that reads the correct frequency and there are no known side effects.

Because a tattoo is visible, it is immediately recognizable and reported when a lost dog is found, which means that tattooing could easily be the most effective means of identification available.

As well, dog thieves are less likely to steal a dog that has a permanent visible form of identification. There are several registries for tattooed dogs, including the National Dog Tattoo Registry in the UK, which has a network of Accredited Tattooists across the UK.

The fee for tattooing and registering a dog for their lifetime is approximately $35(£25).

In the United States, the National Dog Registry (NDR) was founded in 1966 and since then, NDR has supervised, directed, conducted, or overseen the tattooing of more than 6 million animals.

The cost for tattooing a single dog is approximately $10 (£7) plus a one-time registration fee of $45 (£30).

9. Pet Insurance

Pet guardians commonly ask themselves, when considering medical insurance for their dog, whether they can afford not to have it.

On one hand, in light of all the new treatments and medications that are now available for our dogs which usually come with a very high price tag, an increasing number of guardians have decided to add pet insurance to their list of monthly expenses.

On the other hand, some humans believe that placing money into a savings account, in case unforeseen medical treatments are required, makes more sense.

Pet insurance coverage can cost anywhere from $2,000 to $6,000 (£1201 to £3604) over an average lifespan of a dog, and unless your dog is involved in a serious accident, or contracts a life-threatening disease, you may never need to pay out that much for treatment.

Whether you decide to start a savings account for your Border Collie so that you will always have funds available for unforeseen health issues, or you decide to buy a health insurance plan, most dog lovers will go to any lengths to save the life of their beloved companions.

Having access to advanced technological tools and procedures means that our dogs are now being offered treatment options that were once only reserved for humans.

Now, some canine conditions that were once considered fatal, are being treated at considerable costs ranging anywhere between $1,000 and $5,000 (£597 and £2,986) and more.

However, even in the face of rapidly increasing costs of caring for our dogs, owners purchasing pet insurance remain a small minority.

In an effort to increase the number of people buying pet insurance, insurers have teamed with the American Kennel Club and Petco Animal Supplies to offer the insurance. In addition to this, more than 1,600 companies, such as Office Depot and Google, offer pet insurance coverage to their employees as an optional employee benefit.

Even though you might believe that pet insurance will be your savior anytime your dog needs a trip to the vet's office, you really need to be careful when considering an insurance plan, because there are many policies that contain small print excluding certain ages, hereditary or chronic conditions. Unfortunately, most people don't consider pet insurance when their pets are healthy because buying pet insurance means playing the odds, and unless your dog becomes seriously ill, you end up paying for something that may never happen.

However, just like automobile insurance, you can't buy it after you've had that accident. Therefore, since many of us, in today's uncertain economy, may be hard pressed to pay a high veterinarian bill, generally speaking, the alternative of paying monthly pet insurance premiums will provide peace of mind and improved veterinarian care for our best friends.

Shop around, because as with all insurance policies, pet insurance policies will vary greatly between companies and the only way to know for certain exactly what sort of coverage you are buying is to be holding a copy of that policy in your hand so that you can clearly read what will and what will not be covered. Don't forget to carefully read the fine print to avoid any nasty surprises, because the time to discover that a certain procedure will not be covered is not when you are in the middle of filing a claim.

Before Purchasing a Policy

There are several considerations to be aware of before choosing to purchase a pet insurance policy, including:

- Is your dog required to undergo a physical exam?
- Is there a waiting period before the policy becomes active?
- What percentage of the bill does the insurance company pay — after the deductible?
- Are payments limited or capped in any way?
- Are there co-pays (cost to you up front)?
- Does the plan cover pre-existing conditions?
- Does the plan cover chronic or recurring medical problems?
- Can you choose any vet or animal hospital to treat your pet?
- Are prescription medications covered?
- Are you covered when traveling with your pet?
- Does the policy pay if your pet is being treated and then dies?

When you love your dog and worry that you may not have the funds to cover an emergency medical situation that could unexpectedly cost thousands, the right pet insurance policy will provide both peace of mind and better health care for your beloved furry friend.

Chapter 13: Financial Aspects

Owning a Border Collie is not as straightforward as it looks. Taking care of your dog can seriously burn your wallet. Their acquisition costs are quite decent but their constant upkeep and maintenance requires you to incur additional costs. If you are looking for a realistic estimate, here it is!

Prior owners of Border Collie dogs observe that on average, their pet consumes around $1,200 (£820) from their yearly budget! This estimate is a moderate one that you need to spend on your Border Collie dog's upkeep. If you try to be a "giving" master, you can expect these figures to sky-rocket to colossal heights!

1. Food

The primary cost in this figure is the cost of its food – an expense that you need to make in all cases. Border Collie dogs need high quality dry dog food. If you try to put them on people food, they are likely to develop health problems which will end up costing you significantly more than the amount you saved on dog food!

The best ones on the market cost between $40 and $70 (£27 and £45) for a 27-30 pound bag. Depending on the size of your Border Collie dog, this may last a month (if it weighs about 50lbs and consumes roughly 1 pound of food daily) to 10 days (if it weighs about 160 lbs and consumes about 3 pounds of food daily). Simple math can show you how significant this cost amounts up to over the months.

Moreover, this does not include the cost of treats and other supplements you might decide to give to your pet. The treats alone can incur an additional cost up to $20 (£14) for a large bag. Vitamins and other supplements may have varying costs depending on their composition ranging between $10 and $250 (£7 and £170) per bottle. Generally, you do not need to worry about vitamins and supplements if you have a puppy. The same, however, cannot be said for the aged Border Collie dogs.

When it is about taking care of your pet, sky is the only limit to what it may cost you!

2. Accessories

The estimate mentioned above does not include the cost of dog accessories like the travel crate, dog toys and other items of use. Usually these are purchased well in advance and can be used for years at a stretch.

If you are still looking for an estimate, consider this: an average travel crate for your Border Collie puppy can cost between $120 and $200 (£82 and £135)! However, if you settle for a smaller travel crate to accommodate a Border Collie puppy, you will need to buy another one as the puppy grows rapidly into its larger-than-life adulthood! Intelligent choices can save you quite a few bucks.

As far as its grooming is concerned, be ready to spend another couple of hundreds on these accessories. For instance, you can get nail clippers and trimmers for $20 (£13.67) to $60 (£41.01). A regular hair brush can cost you about $15 (£10.25); an organic one would be slightly more expensive. Pet wipes may cost about $20 (£13.67) per pack and medicated shampoos can cost you about the same. If you purchase them all, you may incur a cost of $100 (£68.35) to $150 (£102.53) or more on grooming supplies alone.

If you are taking your Border Collie in for some professional grooming, be ready to spend anywhere between $30 (£20.51) and $50 (£34.17) per visit. Seeing the quality and length of hair that a Border Collie has, it is encouraged for you to take your pet over for professional grooming services at some point or the other.

Collars and leashes are another important expense that can cost you anything between $10 (£6.84) for the most basic accessory to $70 (£47.85) for more stylish equipment with multiple utility. If you decide to add in a couple of flashy identification tags to the collar, you can add in a few more bucks to compensate for that. The purpose served by the $10(£6.84) leash will be more or less the same as that of the $70 (£47.85) one. The only difference is that the latter might offer you options to "fasten" your pet into your car as well.

Dog toys are relatively inexpensive. You can get a bunch of these for $10(£6.84) and they would be durable enough to last six months if not one year! If you go for stuffed toys, the cost may be slightly higher – about $15 (£10.25) for a toy. Nevertheless, these costs are very well justified and contribute a small portion of your overall expenses.

3. The Vet

Your concerns don't end here. There is the annual trip to the veterinary doctor as well that is bound to gouge a significant hole in your financial resources.

It largely depends on the locality you live in. In some place, you can find veterinary services for much cheaper than in other places. On the whole, it can cost you about $250 (£170.88) to $1,000 (£683.5). If you are looking for specialized services like micro chipping, the costs will be significant and charged separately. Any other surgical procedures that your pet needs will incur costs over the given estimate.

The annual checkup costs tend to be larger for two reasons – firstly, you are not making a payment out of your pockets every month; secondly, this cost generally includes the expenses pertaining to blood tests, heartworm tests and several other similar examinations. The cost of yearly vaccinations is also embedded in this cost. Hence the mountainous amount is justified.

Alternatively, if you go for semi-annual checkups, it will cost you about $100 (£68.35) to $150 (£102.53) per visit. The scarcity of such services has contributed towards selective inflation in this segment of medical care. Make sure you check in with your preferred veterinarian beforehand to get a realistic estimate of your yearly budget.

If you settle for a diseased puppy or a disease-prone breed, rest assured your medical care costs will be significantly higher than those mentioned in here. This is also one of the reasons why purchasing registered dogs from authentic breeders is encouraged.

Additionally, the cost of spaying or neutering a Border Collie is also quite high. If you want to get a female dog spayed, it will cost you between $170 (£116.2) and $240 (£164.04). The cost of neutering male Border Collie dogs range between $120 (£82.02) and $175 (£119.61). This is a onetime expenditure and hence should not be a major concern for you. You can also find non-profit charitable organizations in your vicinity to help take care of your pet if the costs are getting too high beyond affordability.

4. Dog Training

And this brings us to another most important financial aspect of petting a dog – the cost of training. This also depends on your locality and if you are lucky you might be able to find certain resources that are more affordable.

On average, a single training class with the training center can cost you between $15 and $45 (£10.25- £30). Group classes average for $150 to $250 (£102.53 -£170.88) for a four to six week schedule respectively. The twist here is this; there are more than a dozen training courses for dogs! Each training course comes at a price. So if you add it all up, you will end up with a figure that may be out of reach.

For this reason, conducting a needs assessment beforehand will be a good option. As an owner, you have the right kind of experience to understand what kind of training your pet needs. Consequently, you can work in collaboration with your local training centers to work on those areas that demand attention. Getting your pet to behave well is definitely a priority as compared with having your pet fetch various things on your order.

If you are unclear about what type of training classes your pet needs in order to improve its responses, you can consult and discuss it with training experts available at the center. They will guide you through the process in the best possible manner while making sure the results you seek are delivered.

5. Miscellaneous Expenses

There are a few other dog accessories – like the dog gates, barriers and other similar installations – for which an estimate has not been included deliberately. It all depends on you – how much you are willing to spend. The more you spend, the more accessories your pet will have. Even though this does not always translate into its happiness, it does mean exaggerated comfort for your beloved canine friend.

Apart from all these costs, you should be prepared for property damage as well when and if the Border Collie dog becomes too agitated to calm down. It can wreck havoc in your living space, tear up the sofas and curtains and is very well equipped to knock down your doors too! Usually training does the trick but it pays to be safe and anticipate the worst even if it isn't happening!

Usually the first year is the hardest and the most expensive. This is the time when your pet is settling in and is therefore going through a number of adjustment issues. So if and when it tries to express its anger or frustration, it can end up costing you a couple of dollars. However, over time, your pet will learn to respect your authority and will therefore make things much easier.

All the figures given in here are estimates. Actual prices of commodities may vary. A range has been given to accommodate the expensive as well as inexpensive options.

In fact, the yearly estimates given above also pertain to situations where you keep away from unnecessary and luxurious expenditures. The more you try to pamper your pet, the higher the total costs will become! Even though your pet does not really understand "money" as much as it understands "love", it will nevertheless like being pampered. For Border Collie dogs, their luxury threshold is reached sooner than most other breeds.

Keeping and maintaining a Border Collie dog is by no means an easy feat. It does not only demand a significant portion of your finances but also an equally exhaustive slice of your time and effort. There is a lot you need to do to make this association work out positively. Although the Border Collie dog is an intelligent learner, it nevertheless will not be able to understand your rules if you do not make a conscious effort to get the right message across.

So do you really have it in you to pet a Border Collie and provide nothing but the best for it?!

Chapter 14: General Tips, Tricks and Guidelines

Here are a few guidelines for taking care of a canine companion in general. Regardless of the breed that you own, you can care for your canine companion in a better way by keeping in mind the following things.

1. Helping the dog Transition

The impending loss of a beloved dog is one of the most painfully difficult and emotionally devastating experiences a canine guardian will ever have to face.

For the sake of our faithful companions, because we do not want to prolong their suffering, we humans will have to do our best to look at our dog's situation practically, rather than emotionally, so that we can make the best decision for them.

They may be suffering from extreme old age and the inability to even walk outside to relieve themselves, and thus having to deal with the indignity of regularly soiling their sleeping area, they may have been diagnosed with an incurable illness that is causing them much pain, or they may have been seriously injured.

Whatever the reason for a canine's suffering, it will be up to their human guardian to calmly guide the end-of-life experience so that any further discomfort and distress can be minimized.

What to Do If You Are Uncertain?

In circumstances where it is not entirely clear how much a dog is suffering, it will be helpful to pay close attention to your Border Collie dog's behavior and keep a daily log or record so that you can know for certain how much of their day is difficult and painful for them, and how much is not.

When you keep a daily log, it will be easier to decide if the dog's quality of life has become so poor that it makes better sense to offer them the gift of peacefully going to sleep.

During this time of uncertainty, it will also be very important to discuss with your veterinarian what signs of suffering may be associated with the dog's particular disease or condition, so that you know what to look for.

Often a dog may still continue to eat or drink despite being upset, having difficulty breathing, excessively panting, being disoriented or in much pain, and as their caring guardians, we will have to weigh their love of eating against how much they are really suffering in all other aspects of their life.

Obviously, if a canine guardian can clearly see that their beloved companion is suffering throughout their days and nights, it will make sense to help humanely end their suffering by planning a euthanasia procedure.

We humans are often tempted to delay the inevitable moment of euthanasia, because we love our dogs so much and cannot bear the anticipation of the intense grief we know will overwhelm us when we must say our final goodbyes to our beloved fur friend.

Unfortunately, we may regret that we allowed our dog to suffer too long, and could find ourselves wishing that if only we humans had the same option, to peacefully let go, when we find ourselves in such a stage in our own lives.

2. Euthanasia – What, Why and How?

Every veterinarian will have received special training to help provide all incurably ill, injured or aged pets that have come to the end of their natural lives with a humane and gentle death, through a process called "euthanasia".

When the time comes, euthanasia, or putting a dog "to sleep", will usually be a two-step process.

First, the veterinarian will inject the dog with a sedative to make them sleepy, calm and comfortable.

Second, the veterinarian will inject a special drug that will peacefully stop their heart.

These drugs work in such a way that the dog will not experience any awareness whatsoever that their life is ending. What they will experience is very much like what we humans experience when falling asleep under anesthesia during a surgical procedure.

Once the second stage drug has been injected, the entire process takes about 10 to 20 seconds, at which time the veterinarian will then check to make certain that the dog's heart has stopped.

There is no suffering with this process, which is a very gentle and humane way to end a dog's suffering and allow them to peacefully pass on.

3. Where Most Dog/Puppy Owners Go Wrong

Here are some of the common mistakes made by people while petting their canine companions. Make sure you are not one of them as this can seriously disrupt your relationship with your Border Collie dog at some point in time or the other!

Experimentation

First and foremost, you should not experiment with your pet, especially in matters pertaining to its health.

Self-medication is the last thing you should do even if your pet seems to have developed a problem that had occurred previously. You might be inclined to do so in order to save some costs but do keep in mind the dog doesn't respond to medication in the same way as humans.

If and when you plan backfires, the results will be even more drastic!

Sleeping in Your Bed

Many of us humans make the mistake of allowing a crying puppy to sleep in their bed, and while this may help to calm and comfort a new puppy, it will set a dangerous precedent that can result in behavioral problems later in their life.

As much as it may pull on your heart strings to hear your new Border Collie puppy crying the first couple of night in their kennel, a little tough love at the beginning will keep them safe while helping them to learn to both love and respect you as their leader.

Picking Them Up at the Wrong Time

Never pick your puppy up if they display nervousness, fear or aggression (such as growling) toward an object, person or other pet, because this will be rewarding them for unbalanced behavior.

Instead, your puppy needs to be gently corrected by you, with firm and calm energy so that they learn not to react with fear or aggression.

Playing Too Hard or Too Long

Many humans play too hard or allow their children to play too long or too roughly with a young puppy.

You need to remember that a young puppy tires very easily and especially during the critical growing phases of their young life, they need their rest.

Hand Play

Always discourage your Border Collie puppy from chewing or biting your hands, or any part of your body for that matter.

If you allow them to do this when they are puppies, they will want to continue to do so when they have strong jaws and adult teeth and this is not acceptable behavior for any breed of dog.

Do not get into the habit of playing the "hand" game, where you rough up the puppy and slide them across the floor with your hands, because this will teach your puppy that your hands are playthings.

When your puppy is teething, they will naturally want to chew on everything within reach, and this will include you. As cute as you might think it is, this is not an acceptable behavior and you need to gently, but firmly, discourage the habit.

A light flick with a finger on the end of a puppy nose, combined with a firm "NO" when they are trying to bite human fingers will discourage them from this activity.

Not Getting Used to Grooming

Not taking the time to get your Border Collie used to a regular grooming routine, including bathing, brushing, toenail clipping and teeth brushing can lead to a lifetime of trauma for both human and dog every time these procedures must be performed.

Set aside a few minutes each day for your grooming routine.

Get your Border Collie used to being up high, on a table or countertop when you are grooming them, because when it comes time for a full grooming session, then they will not be stressed by being placed on a grooming table.

Free Feeding

Free feeding means to keep food in your puppy's bowl 24/7 so that they can eat any time of the day or night, whenever they feel like it.

While free feeding a young puppy can be a good idea until they are about four or five months old, many guardians of different breeds often get into the bad habit of allowing their adult dogs to continue to eat food any time they want, by leaving food out 24/7.

This can be a serious mistake, as your Border Collie needs to know that you are absolutely in control of their food.

If your Border Collie does not associate the food they eat with you, they may become picky eaters or think that they are the boss, which can lead to other behavioral issues later in life.

So be intelligent about your Border Collie decision right from the beginning. You are about to create a rewarding relationship with your pet – don't spoil it by making the wrong decisions right at the start!

Extraordinary Creation

You should not consider it as an extraordinary being of any sort. It cannot take care of itself, cannot recognize what may be lethal for it and definitely cannot be expected to adapt or adjust to different settings.

It is not human, and you being its owner are responsible for keeping it healthy. Don't be negligent about your pet's needs – you never know when you might end up harming your own pal.

Being Too Distracted

If you have too many distractions to keep you busy through days or nights, are planning to have a child of your own, are one of the laid back types or simply cannot devote time and attention to your pet for whatever reason, it is best to stay away from such a commitment.

Border Collie dogs demand more effort as compared to other breeds. If you cannot keep up with its pace, well then don't get involved!

No Need for Training

Besides this, never be misled into believing your Border Collie dog is naturally well-behaved or does not need training because it seems to be doing very well without it.

Border Collie dogs learn quickly and will therefore follow your orders easily. However, it wouldn't be long before its internal state of crisis will get into the way of obedience.

Start training the Border Collie dog as early as possible to make sure that unfortunate occurrences can be kept to a bare minimum.

The more you delay training for your Border Collie dog, the more stubborn and irresponsive it will become. So it is in your best interest not to procrastinate this duty.

Inconsistent Orders

On the same note, make sure you (and your family) use consistent words for specific actions.

Your Border Collie is not a human and will therefore become extremely confused if you use the same word and expect it to act differently. Even if it is impulsively and linguistically right, the same cannot be said for your pet's understanding.

Consider this for example; if you want it to sit on the floor, you say "down" and when your spouse wants it off the sofa, they say "down". It will become worse when your kid says "down" to get the Border Collie dog down a flight of stairs.

Linguistically, the word is used correctly in all three situations. But it is creating confusion in the mind of the Border Collie about what the owner(s) wants.

It is best to use separate words for different actions and then reinforce this definition to make sure your Border Collie dog respond well.

Not Using Enough Treats

It is recommended to use treats often, especially during the training phase. It is easily the best way to reinforce actions and responses.

So whenever your pet follows your orders or responds to the most recent training class, treat it with some snacks. It will know when it is being praised and will therefore respond to make you happy.

Loosing Temper

What would you do if your Border Collie dog fails to perform the way you want it to?

Whatever you do, don't shout, holler or physically hurt it. Your Border Collie dog is not a puppet that will follow your orders perfectly every time.

Making mistakes every now and then is perfectly normal for this animal. It will take time and patience to train your Border Collie dog and have it follow your wishes. It does not happen overnight.

So if you are under the impression that training sessions begin yielding results right away, clear the misconception before penalizing your pet.

Leaving it off the Leash

Never try to leave your Border Collie off the leash until and unless you are absolutely sure it is well disciplined. Although it is encouraged to conduct your training sessions in public areas or in places where numerous distractions exist, make sure you do so once your pet has understood the basics.

Training amidst distractions makes sure your pet responds to your orders in similar situations. But if you leave it off the leash before training sessions take effect, it is more likely to wander off to restricted territories, bite a few people or animals and get you into a lot of trouble that could have been avoided if you kept the leash intact!

Leaving it Unattended

Lastly and most importantly, don't let your pet get lonely or leave it unsupervised for long time periods.

It is a disastrous combination which can result in all sorts of damage – to your property as well as your pet. A lonely Border Collie is likely to experiment with different objects within the house. Such activities are not always uneventful.

Also, don't leave it unsupervised in a place where known threats exist. For instance, don't keep it locked in the car or leave it at a park without supervision. Such negligence may end up inflicting irreversible harm to your pet.

Expecting too much!

Don't expect too much from your pet in too little time. Patience and perseverance is the key to success. Let your Border Collie dog settle in and absorb your rules – it will eventually get there. Haste can only make matters worse for you as well as for your newfound pet!

Understanding Its Body Language

It can prove to be a big mistake to automatically assume that if the dog is wagging its tail, it is doing so because it is happy and/or friendly.

When determining the dog's true intent or demeanor, you need to take into consideration the entire body posture of the dog because it is highly possible that a dog can be wagging its tail just before it decides to take an aggressive lunge towards you.

More important in determining the emotional state of a dog is the height or positioning of its tail.

For instance, a tail that is held parallel to the dog's back usually suggests that the dog is feeling relaxed, whereas, if the tail is held stiffly vertical, this usually means that the dog is feeling aggressive or dominant.

A tail held much lower can mean that the dog is feeling stressed, afraid, submissive or unwell and if the tail is tucked underneath the dog's body, this is most often a sign that the dog is feeling fearful and threatened by another dog or person.

Paying attention to your dog's tail can help you to know when you need to step in and make some space between your dog and another dog.

Of course, different breeds naturally carry their tails at different heights, so you will need to take this into consideration when studying your dog's tail so that you get used to their particular signals.

As well, the speed the tail is moving will also give you an idea of the mental state of the dog because the speed of the wag usually indicates how excited a dog may be.

For instance, a slow, slightly swinging wag can often mean that the dog is tentative about greeting another dog, and this is more of a questioning type of wag, whereas a fast moving tail held high can mean that a dog is about to challenge or threaten another dog.

Interestingly, two veterinarians at the University of Bari and a neuroscientist at the University of Trieste, in Italy, published a paper in which their research outlined that dogs' tails wagged more to their right side when they had positive feelings about a person or situation, and more to the left side when they were feeling negative.

While certainly a dog's tail can help humans to understand how our dogs might be feeling, there are many other factors to take into consideration when determining your dog's state of mind.

Simply looking at the tail to gauge its mood is therefore not recommended!

4. Caring for Aged Dogs

Caring for an aging dog is slightly different from caring for a puppy. Their demands and needs are infinitely different. It is

154

common to come across one if you are involved in rescuing the Border Collie breed. Here are some of the things you need to keep in mind while handling aged Border Collies.

Aged Border Collie dogs, especially if they come from battered homes, are likely to have several health issues. Make sure you keep these in mind while preparing their meals and activities.

It is advised not to serve them any hard foods or bones that can damage their gums. Also, keep the oil content in foods low so that digestive issues can be kept to a minimum.

On this note, keep in mind that some of the health problems faced by your Border Collie dog are likely to come naturally with age. There is no way to delay or eliminate these.

For instance, most aged dogs will experience impaired hearing and sight over time. Learn to differentiate between imminent dangers and the natural course of life.

Your veterinary doctor is more skilled to tell you about the different signs likely to be exhibited by your pet. However, it pays to consider anything out of the ordinary as a potential threat for your pet's well-being!

Aged Border Collie dogs are not likely to be as energetic as young ones. Plan their activities in a placid manner.

Remember to take them out for walks and other activities as it helps prevent the arthritis from becoming a major problem.

Select a peaceful space in your house where they can rest through the day. You can take them for rides but beware of their stress urinary incontinence.

Don't forget the annual checkups. Better still increase its frequency to semi-annually.

As far as the vaccinations are concerned, ask your veterinary doctor if it is advisable to tune down the frequency to once every three years.

Besides this, you might need to use some vitamins and supplements to counter failing health. The rest all should be fine.

5. *Tackling their Natural Demise*

Some humans do not fully recognize the terrible grief involved in losing a beloved canine friend.

There will be many who do not understand the close bond humans can have with our dogs, which is often unlike any we have with our human counterparts.

Your friends may give you pitying looks and try to cheer you up, but if they have never experienced such a loss themselves, they may also secretly think that you are making too much fuss over "just a dog".

For some of us humans, the loss of a beloved dog is so painful that we decide never to share our lives with another, because we cannot bear the thought of going through the pain of loss again.

Expect to feel terribly sad, tearful and yes, depressed because those who are close to their canine companions will feel the pain no less than losing a human friend or life partner.

The grieving process can take some time to recover from, and some of us never totally recover.

After the loss of a family dog, first you need to take care of yourself by making certain that you keep eating and getting regular sleep, even though you will feel an almost eerie sense of loneliness.

Losing a beloved dog is a shock to the system, which can also affect your concentration and your ability to find joy or want to participate in other activities that may be part of your daily life.

During this time, you will need to take extra care while driving or performing tasks that require your concentration as you may find yourself distracted.

If there are other dogs or pets in the home, they will also be grieving the loss of a companion, and may display this by acting depressed, being off their food or showing little interest in play or games. Therefore, you need to help guide your other pets through this grieving process by keeping them busy and interested, taking them for extra walks and spending more time with them.

6. Adopting a dog

Many people do not wait long enough before replacing a lost pet and immediately go to a local shelter to adopt a deserving dog.

While this may help to distract you from your grieving process, this is not really fair to the new fur member of your family.

Bringing a new pet into a home that is depressed and grieving the loss of a long time canine member may create behavioral problems for the new dog that will be faced with learning all about their new home while also dealing with the unstable, sad energy of the grieving family.

A better scenario would be to allow yourself the time to properly grieve by waiting a minimum of one month to allow yourself and your family to feel happier and more stable before deciding upon sharing your home with another dog.

The grieving process will be different for everyone and you will know when the time is right to consider sharing your home with another canine companion.

Conclusion

Before adopting a Border Collie, it is recommended that you have prior experience of owning a pet. Being a fair disciplinarian while being firm at the same time is what is required of you when dealing with a pet.

Border Collies are extremely hyper and playful. Therefore, it becomes important that the owner has the ability to maintain the same levels of energy as it will allow them to keep up with the Border Collie.

Even though Border Collies are intelligent, your commitment towards their training is essential if you desire a well behaved dog. Border Collies are medium sized dogs with an average height between 17 to 23 inches and weighing between 30 to 55 pounds.

They are a multi-colored breed, including black and red tri-color, blue merle, red & white, sable and black & white. The coat of the Collie can be anything from short and smooth to long, feathered and curvy.

As Border Collies manage to stay relatively clean, minimal grooming is required for them. However, trimming their toe nails, brushing their coat and bathing is required time to time. Border Collies generally stay away from dirt and do not require trimming of coat often.

A simply incredible breed of dog is the Border Collie. A highly intelligent dog, Border Collie can sense what you're thinking and feeling by simply looking at your face. Border Collies pout continuously for a long period of time as they're highly sensitive dogs and get their feeling easily hurt.

Affection is a word synonymous with Border Collies as they're level of attachment to their owner is extreme. Border Collies would want you to play with them all the time as they're known to be extremely playful dogs.

Being close to their owners, watching television, swimming and travelling is what Border Collies enjoy the most. The best thing about Border Collies is that they perform two extremes really well. They have the ability to run and play for hours as well as the ability to sit down and rest at one place for hours.

You will love owning a Border Collie if you're an outdoor and adventurous person meaning you spend more time outdoors than you do inside your house.

Also you're in luck with a Collie if you're an innovative person and want to teach it some tricks that have never been heard of as it is an extremely intelligent dog that learns fast.

If you are an easy going person then a Border Collie may not be the right dog for you. On the other hand, a Border Collie is perfect for you if you expect attention, affection and devotion from your dog.

On the whole it is considered to be an amiable dog – with friends as well as foes. It is therefore considered as one of the best dog breeds to own.

We wish you a happy companionship with your Border Collie!

Published by IMB Publishing 2015

16577021R00090

Printed in Great Britain
by Amazon